The Last Years of British Rail 1985-89

John Stretton

• BRITISH RAILWAYS COLLECTION •
from
The NOSTALGIA Collection

First published by Silver Link Publishing as part of *Closely Observed Trains* in 1994
This edition first published 2005

British Library Cataloguing in Publication Data

A catalogue record for this book is available from the British Library.

ISBN 1 85794 219 1

Silver Link Publishing Ltd
The Trundle
Ringstead Road
Great Addington
Kettering
Northants NN14 4BW

Tel/Fax: 01536 330588
email: sales@nostalgiacollection.com
Website: www.nostalgiacollection.com

Printed and bound in Great Britain

Frontispiece A sight that is fast disappearing from much of our railway system: once a common feature of the railway landscape – at least externally – many signal boxes were swept away during the 1980s, with little ceremony and largely maintaining the momentum of the previous two or three decades. One such casualty was the box at Syston North Junction, seen here on 1 March 1987, a mere five weeks before closure and demolition. Note the armchair and spotless floor and lever frame in this view looking north. *MJS*

Acknowledgements

A s with the other two volumes in this series of books, I am indebted to the small coterie of photographers who have helped me with the project. They are basically the same four that assisted me with the compilation of *Closely Observed Trains*, which looked at BR in the 1980s and from which this new edition has evolved. Their continued co-operation, assistance, support and encouragement is valued more than they are aware. I am also grateful to David Holmes, for his contribution to this volume, and to the publishers for the loan of some of Ray Ruffell's photographs from their library. In addition, my heartfelt thanks go to Brian Morrison for his efforts in proofreading and coping with my tight deadlines! How he managed to fit it all in between his other multifarious duties and demands, I shall never know. The illustrations credited 'MJS' are mine.

As usual, credit and huge thanks must go to my wife Judi, who tolerates long periods of isolation, or me like a bear with a sore head, as I either sit huddled gnome-like in front of the computer or peer at innumerable photographs. Without her continued forbearance, I could not have achieved the task – albeit slightly behind deadline! Finally, thanks to all at Silver Link – Peter for encouragement and for putting up with countless phone calls; David for his unflinching patience and courtesy; and to Will and Mick for their usual skilful and speedy editing and design. Thank you all.

Contents

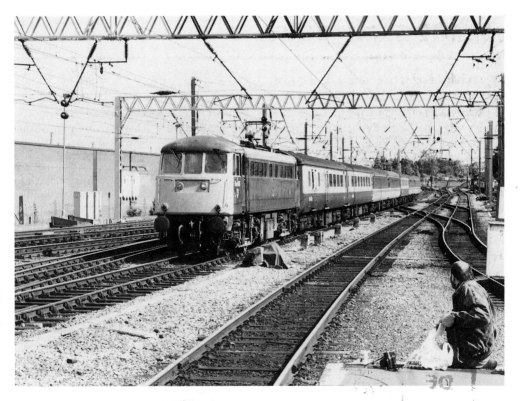

The West Coast Main Line (WCML) electrification during the 1960s brought new types of motive power to the route, but 20 years later many of the earlier examples were reaching the end of their active lives. By the end of the decade, Classes 82, 83 and 84 were extinct and the majority of 81s and 85s had also been withdrawn from front-line service. In this view on 1 June 1989, No 85015, one of the few remaining active class members, fights a rearguard action against abandonment, deputising for a failed loco as it heads into Carlisle station, 20 minutes late, with the 0845 Brighton-Glasgow/Edinburgh 'Sussex Scot'. The end came 15 months later, from Crewe Electric depot on 8 September 1990. Note the modern-day spotter, complete with camera and bag of sandwiches. *MJS*

Introduction

So there is no confusion or doubt, let me state at the outset that this volume is a new edition of the second half of *Closely Observed Trains*, published by Silver Link in 1994 but now long out of print. Some of the illustrations may therefore be familiar, but, perhaps more importantly, there are many new ones and the captions to the 'originals' have been revised and updated.

Much has happened over the ten years or so since the original volume saw the light of day and I have taken the opportunity to reflect on the period under consideration with the benefit of hindsight since Privatisation in 1995. Wherever possible I have attempted to bring the story up to date. With the two complementary volumes, covering 1980-84 and 1990-94, the series presents a fascinating look at the last 15 years of British Rail, a period that possibly saw as much change in the fortunes of our railways as any other previous similar period.

As the half-decade covered by this current volume closed, we had endured 20 years since the end of steam on BR. We had lived through the 'Corporate Blue' period of the 1970s/early 1980s – when so many photographers simply hung up their camera bags! – and had entered Sectorisation and a proliferation of multi-coloured liveries. Classes of locomotive continued to become extinct, with new ones emerging, though fewer in number with the spread of DMU/EMU units replacing loco-hauled trains. BR Works also suffered, with the infamous closure of Swindon at the same time as celebrating GW150 being perhaps the most heartless. Politically, the climate was still not pro-railways, with inevitable consequences.

It was also the period that saw the electrification of the ECML, the death of Dr Beeching, the last locos to leave Dai Woodham's yard on Barry Docks, the launch of Network SouthEast and the end of Cornish Railways, the saving of Marylebone and the Settle-Carlisle line from closure, the launch of six new Railfreight identities, the closure of the 'Leicester Gap' but the re-opening of Birmingham Snow Hill station, and the setting of a new world diesel speed record – utilising power cars 43109 and 43118 on the ECML. So, as can be seen, there was much going on in and around our railways in the period covered by this book. I suspect that much will have been unknown to many at the time or forgotten by even more since, and I hope, therefore, that the images and comments within these pages will either educate you afresh or reunite you with past memories. I also hope it will encourage you to immerse yourself in the current railway, as today's vision is tomorrow's half-remembered experience.

I have thoroughly enjoyed 'going back in time' and wallowing in nostalgia, and I hope that you will equally enjoy this journey. The images have been chosen as much for their aesthetic quality as their intrinsic historic value. We are fortunate that there were – and still are – skilful, dedicated and energetic photographers, who thought nothing of travelling the length and breadth of the UK capturing images on film. If you have not tried it, I can recommend the experience – and, nowadays, with digital, there are no film costs! So, go out and enjoy yourselves!

The art of railway photography is more than just 'point and shoot', especially in the modern era, without the inherent benefit of steam! Increasingly, with standardisation and the predominance of multiple units, the aesthetics and composition have to be right before putting a train in the picture. This photographer has never been afraid to take chances, see things in a slightly different way, often to great effect. An example of his style is here displayed, showing 'Sprinter' No 150235 on the approaches to Shrewsbury, at Sutton Bridge, operating as the 1004 Cardiff-Manchester 'Cross Country' service. *Tom Heavyside*

On a brief 'escape' from a Ten-Pin Bowling Tour of the north with Barclays Bank, I spent some time at Leeds City station on 14 March 1985, enjoying the glorious sunshine. Among the delights was this Met-Cam twin-car Class 111 DMU, comprising E54092 and 53135, standing in Platform 6 as empty coaching stock, after arriving from Wakefield (Westgate). Renumbered from Nos 56092 and 50135 respectively, both entered service in April 1957. The former was withdrawn 30 years later, in June 1987, and cut up at Mayer Newman's Snailwell yard exactly a year later. No 53135 was withdrawn from squadron service in November 1987, to go on to further useful service as Departmental No 977539 until it also met its fate at Mayer Newman's in August 1989. *MJS*

26 January

Looking back over the past 20 years, the WCML has seen much change, not least in political fortunes. Much controversy has surrounded the millions of pounds spent on the various plans for upgrade and modernisation, and in many ways the service has been transformed – not wholly positively, however! In a period when the status quo seemed to be permanent on this route to Scotland, No 86255 *Penrith Beacon* is attractively framed by trees and branches as it climbs towards Shap Summit, at Greenholme with the 1022 train from Birmingham to Glasgow/Edinburgh. The former No 86042, this loco, like its classmates, was ousted from front-line duties by the onset of Virgin's 'Pendolinos' in the early years of the 21st century and was put into store. *Tom Heavyside*

▲ 16 February

Another skilful use by this photographer of conditions, surroundings and ambient light: the snow, side-lighting, framing and judicious positioning of the arriving Class 116 DMU turn a potentially ordinary shot into a very pleasing one. The silhouettes of tree trunk and foliage and lamp standards 'ancient and modern' on either side beautifully frame unpretentious Cardiff set C313 as it is led by DMS 53900 entering Stroud on a Gloucester-Swindon local service. Note how the passengers are still graced with a forward view at this time. *Tom Heavyside*

▼ 12 March

Too far away to eavesdrop on their conversation, the two railwaymen add to the detritus on the platform and in the 'four-foot', together with the serpentine temporary and permanent fencing and station superstructure, to make for a pleasing portrait. Yet another image captured during the above-mentioned northern Ten-Pin Bowling tour, Parcels Van No M55993 stands in one of the terminal platforms at Manchester Victoria. In all-'Corporate Blue' at this time, it was destined to be transformed into Post Office red three or four years later. New in February 1960, it was withdrawn in November 1990 and cut up at MC Metals' Glasgow yard five months later. *MJS*

▲ 16 March

The destination blind states 'Shaw via Oldham' and this places us unequivocally on the ex-L&YR 'circular' route from Manchester Victoria to Rochdale via Shaw & Crompton. In weak late-winter sunshine, the driver, complete with peaked cap, takes his twin-coach charge, with BRCW Class 104 No M53468 at the front, through bleak countryside at Heyside, nearing its destination as the 1600 service from Victoria. Into the 21st century the route was initially closed to accommodate conversion to Metro services, but funding was then refused by the SRA! Having given reliable service, with very little alteration since construction, the former No 50468 unit managed to celebrate its 30th birthday before withdrawal in September 1989; the end came at Vic Berry's Leicester yard just three months later. *Tom Heavyside*

▼ 28 March

Semaphore signalling has been a strategic feature and has improved countless railway photographs, this gantry at the southern exit from Taunton station being sadly missed when it was dismantled not so long after this view. GUV ('General Utility Van') trains have also since gone the way of all flesh but, thankfully, they did survive the decade under examination. No 47306 – named *Goshawk* at Tinsley depot on 20 December 1989 – here at the head of the 0505 Paddington-Plymouth van train, also survived into the 1990s and beyond. Changing its name to *The Sapper*, at Stratford-upon-Avon on 22 April 1994, it was still nominally in service 20 years on from this view, but in store. *Brian Morrison*

31 March

In another example of this photographer's skill in making a mundane scene more interesting, who would have thought of capturing this scene with the train such a small element and with the 'Offers Invited' sign balancing the prominent lamp standard on the left? Yet the rows of houses are important to the overall effect and superbly lead the eye to the ultimate focus of viaduct and train. The day is a Sunday – and early morning judging by the absence of humanity! A typical engineer's train of the day rests on Tonge Viaduct in Bolton, on the ex-L&YR line to Blackburn, behind the clean lines of No 45072. Sadly, this was to be one of the November 1961-vintage 45's last duties, being withdrawn from Toton depot just 26 days after this view. It then became another casualty of Vic Berry's yard, disappearing by December 1986. *Tom Heavyside*

▶ 6 April

This year saw a shift of thinking within BR hierarchy away from the all-pervading drab blue 'Corporate' livery, to a more enlightened approach, mirroring the increased attention in society to image and colour. The shift was slow at first, disguising the plethora of rainbow colour/livery changes that were soon to overwhelm us. Here No 86253 *The Manchester Guardian* slows on the entrance to Watford Junction, ready to draw to a halt with the 1006 Euston-Manchester Piccadilly train. Note that the loco is in the early form of InterCity livery, whereas the coaches are still in the blue and grey uniform. Previously numbered 86044, it was again renumbered on 16 December 2004, to 86901, one of two of the class redesigned for Network Rail and resplendent in that company's all yellow livery. *MJS*

▶ 9 April

Alas, the 'Marlow Donkey' is not what it once was! Originating in steam days, the name stuck for the shuttle service to and from Maidenhead, here represented by two single DMU cars. The unit does try to inject some interest into the image with its 'cow horn' exhaust system, but it does not have the inherent appeal of the steam push-pull arrangement. With his hand on the brake, the driver of Class 121 'bubblecar' No W55030 brings one of the shuttles into Bourne End station, now 'terminalised' behind the photographer but once on a through route to High Wycombe. The train will then reverse and take the branch to the right in the background, to travel on to its destination at Marlow. *MJS*

▶ 10 April

Before the project was abandoned, I wanted to witness and photograph the operation of the APT. On a few days' holiday, I tracked down the times of its test run and on this day travelled the relatively short journey from my home in Amersham and set up on Tring station to wait. Short of available free time, due to domestic and parental duties, I liaised with the station

attendant, who kept me appraised of its journey from the north. It was late and I had to abandon my attempt, only to see it roar through the station as I drove away! However, I was compensated during my wait with this view of a Class 81, then becoming very much rarer on main-line working. With just three vans and a coach in tow, No 81005 does not seem to be overburdened on an up parcels train, passing through the station at around 1300. *MJS*

▲ 10 April

Later that day I returned to Tring, but arrived close to the time the APT was due back, so decided not to take any chances and to visit the road overbridge south of the station. A wise decision it proved to be, as the tilting train was approaching as I arrived! I had no time other than to point the camera through the car side window, without so much as metering or focusing! Admittedly it is not a brilliantly composed result, but is the only photograph I have of the APT working and not too bad, all things considered! *MJS*

▼ 11 April

For a good 20 years Class 27s gave sterling service in Scotland but, sadly, did not survive to the end of our decade. Happily though, while many went towards donating materials for baked-bean cans, some did escape the cutter's torch to see further life in preservation. One such was No 27059 – the former D5410, 27123 and 27205! – which survived withdrawal from Eastfield on 6 July 1987 to give pleasure to enthusiasts on the Severn Valley Railway. Here it is running as train engine, with classmate 27026 as pilot, providing 'super power' for a short rake of empty bitumen tanks from Culloden through Blair Atholl station, on the old Highland Railway Perth-Inverness route. *Tom Heavyside*

23 April

The former LNWR branch from Nuneaton to Wigston, just south of Leicester, has seen many changes, both in motive power and levels of service, since its opening in 1864. Narborough station, close to the Leicester end of the branch, was actually closed on 4 March 1968, but such was the outcry from locals that re-opening was achieved within two years, on 5 January 1970. This apart, the line has always been important for both freight and occasional WCML diversions and remains so into the 21st century. On this day, Brush Type 4 motive power has been delegated to haul this afternoon eastbound mixed freight, seen approaching the level crossing by the station platform ends, on the edge of the village. New in August 1965, No 47211 became 47394 on 28 March 1994, was named *Johnson Stevens Agencies* at Tinsley depot on 29 May, reverted to 47211 on 4 September 1995, lost the name on 24 November of that year, and was withdrawn, from Derby Fragonset's books, on 18 October 2003. *Ray Ruffell*

24 April

If you can be persuaded to turn your photographic eye from the standard front three-quarter view – and can, further, include and use the neighbouring infrastructure – you can create some memorable shots, especially if the sun is shining. Ace transport photographer Brian Morrison is a past master at this technique and has here captured a delightful study of a tablet exchange at Tunbridge Wells West B signal box. The warm spring weather has tempted the signalman to be in shirt sleeves, adding to the effect, as DEMU No 1305 is about to pass the box forming the 1457 Eridge-Tonbridge service. *Brian Morrison*

▲ 27 April

Except for the rake of blue and white coaches in tow, this view could almost date from any period following Nationalisation in 1948 – and shows just what can be achieved in preservation with just a little effort and co-operation. Ex-LNER green-liveried 'A4' No 60009 *Union of South Africa* – resplendent with a 64B Haymarket shedplate but perhaps just a little too clean for the purists! – heads past Edinburgh's Princes Street Gardens on one of a series of round trips around the city via the suburban line. *Tom Heavyside*

▼ 29 April

Over the two and a half decades from 1980, both diesel and electric multiple units have ousted locomotives from front-line passenger duties, moving many good engines to premature withdrawal. There were occasions, however, when either due to a shortage of units or a failure, a loco and coaches were substituted. Here No 50041 *Bulwark* is undertaking such a turn, making an attractive vision while passing Par with the 1635 Plymouth-Penzance stopper. Built in October 1968, for the WCML, it was given its name at Laira on 8 May 1978 and handled express duties on both ex-GWR and ex-SR routes to the West before condemnation, again at Laira, on 17 April 1990. *Colin Marsden*

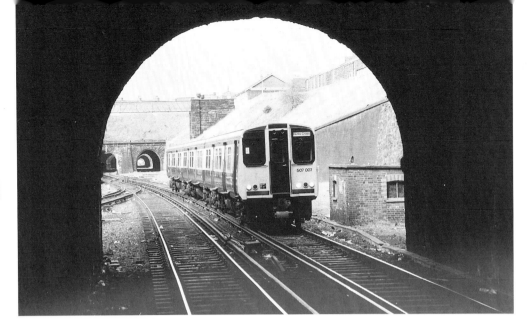

▲ 1 May

With the spread of units replacing locos and stock, the challenge was to make photographs of them aesthetically pleasing. Here the photographer has cleverly utilised the short tunnel on the approach to Kirkdale station to form an attractive archway surround to No 507007, as it slows for the station stop, operating as the 1631 Kirkby-Hunts Cross local. *Tom Heavyside*

▼ 3 May

Once again this photographer has conspired to fully use the available infrastructure to present a real portrait rather than a mere snapshot. Tunnels and cuttings can present problems for photographers, but the potential for success is well encapsulated in this view of No 47409 entering Liverpool Lime Street station with the 1000 'Trans-Pennine' service from Scarborough. Four months later, at King's Cross on 14 September, this engine was named *David Lloyd George* by David Penhaligan MP prior to working a Pullman special to the Liberal Party Assembly at Dundee. The distinction was to be short-lived, however, as the 23-year-old loco was withdrawn from Gateshead depot on 31 August 1986. It was yet another victim of Vic Berry's oxy-acetylene. *Tom Heavyside*

▲ 1 June

Depot Open Days have long been popular public and fundraising events. The Reading event on this day was no exception, and as well as displaying all manner of visual delights, it was graced with brilliantly sunny and hot weather. Encapsulating some of the more unorthodox views, especially for the general public, are No 31158 – showing off the depot's hoist and wearing the then fairly new Railfreight livery, launched without ceremony a mere three months earlier – and a Ballast regulator. *MJS*

▼ 16 June

By the middle of the year the Victoria-Gatwick 'Railair' link had become well established and increasingly popular, with an impressive non-stop service to the airport every 15 minutes, into a dedicated platform at the southern terminal. For the launch of the service, Class 73s were allocated and re-liveried. No 73122 – named *County of East Sussex* exactly one month later, at Lewes – is here seen in a revised 'Executive' livery waiting at Victoria to form the 1600 service to Gatwick. Earmarked to be the reserve Royal '73', sharing duties with No 73142 *Broadlands*, No 73122 had disgraced itself earlier in 1985 by derailing up to its bogies in ballast at Eastbourne! *MJS*

18 July
Oh, the things that we took for granted and now wish we could see again! Still largely unsung at the time, the '45s' were approaching their latter days and were no longer first-call main-line traction. They still performed commendably, however, and were great favourites with both crews and enthusiasts. The porter on Totnes, however, seems totally uninterested in what is about to pass him! No 45141 powers south at the head of a ten-coach rake, the 1V81 0917 Leeds-Penzance holiday service. Although not surviving the decade – being withdrawn from Tinsley on 4 August 1988 – the loco was nevertheless adorned with an unofficial *Zephyr* name at that same depot on 13 August 1987. Note, once more, how setting the train in its surroundings has added to the impact of the image. *Brian Morrison*

▲ 21 July

New Mills was once an important junction to the south-east of Manchester: northwards there were branches to Hayfield and through Strines and Marple; almost due east was the Hope Valley route to Sheffield; and south the ex-LNWR branch to Buxton. Sadly, only the latter two routes still serve the public and the station is not normally graced with the apparently healthy quantity of waiting passengers seen here. The driver of Class 114 Driving Trailer No E54009, at the head of a train from Sheffield, must have wondered at his popularity on this day, but appearances are deceptive, as the vast majority are members of a special party from Buxton awaiting their return trip! The semaphores, roadbridge, footbridges and station canopy all add to the appeal.

▼ 21 July

The travellers having been returned to Buxton, the former LNWR station – something of a Mecca for DMU enthusiasts in the mid-1980s – once again drifts towards a somnolent peace, a siesta to be enjoyed in the warm summer sunshine before the next services are due. Set BX486 (with Class 104 DMS No M53427 nearest the camera) stands empty as back-up, should one be called for, while BX480 (right, with another 104, No M53474, prominent) stands at ease until the next turn. Both cars were withdrawn by the end of the decade, in March 1989, and scrapped by Vic Berry the same month! To the left, one of Buxton's snowploughs can be seen, evidence of the severity of winter weather in these parts. *Both MJS*

▼ 24 July

Like so many other stations throughout the UK, Leicester (London Road) saw great change in the 1970s/80s, not just with the constant change of motive power, but also in its design and standards of passenger comfort and facilities. Some of the change can be witnessed in this view of No 47531 restarting an up parcels train at precisely 0712, with the metal posts on the right being the sole remains at the southern end of this platform of the previous cavernous trainshed. The whole length of the station was opened out, relieving the pervading gloom that was such a part of the previous scene here, but in the process greatly reducing protection from the elements! The Brush Class 4 had quite a history. New in May 1964 as D1584 (from Crewe) and allocated to Landore depot, it moved around the Western Region in quick succession up to the end of steam in 1968. It should have received TOPS number 47021, but instead was graced with 47531 in May 1974, becoming 47974 on 11 June 1990 and reverting on 24 June 1992, by which time it had acquired the name *The Permanent Way Institution*. This

was removed in June 1992, to be replaced in July 1993 by *Respite*. December 1993 saw it again renumbered, to 47775, and it clung to life into the 21st century, albeit in store. *Horace Gamble*

▶ 1 August

During the 1980s the former GWR Paddington-Birmingham/Birkenhead main line via High Wycombe exclusively used DMUs on passenger services – with one exception! This was a daily Wolverhampton-Paddington and return service that was loco-hauled. For the two years that I worked in Flackwell Heath, on the outskirts of High Wycombe, I contrived to see the morning train as often as possible on my way to work. If the 0622 ex-Wolverhampton was on time, I was able to capture it on its exit from Wycombe and still manage to scramble into work on time! The rising gradient southwards made for hard work from the engines and the sound of the '50s' climbing the bank was a delight to savour. Here No 50015 *Valiant* leans into the camber at Loudwater, still accelerating, determined not to lose time. *MJS*

▶ 6 August

In common with Leicester, seen above, Holyhead has undergone much change. Services have come and gone, as have types of motive power and thoughts regarding through trains to London, while the station and its surroundings have also succumbed to changing fashions and notions of progress. Loco-hauled passenger trains just managed to survive past 2000, but had mostly been replaced within four years. In

happier times, No 47463 stands in one of the remaining platforms at precisely 1244, with just 2 minutes to go before it makes the long run across Anglesey and along the North Wales coast before turning south for Crewe and, ultimately, Euston. Note the massive bulk of the ship in the left distance and the infrastructure on the right, much of which has since disappeared. *David Holmes*

21 August

Here's a virtually timeless view at Boston Docks, although the need for a lick of paint on the level crossing gate shows that it has been there for some years and the lattice signal post (ex-GNR?) also indicates a long pedigree. The diminutive crossing box on the right completes the picture, which shows what gems from the past could still be unearthed in the latter years of the 20th century, despite earnest attempts to modernise and upgrade our railway system.

Slightly later in the day, yet more evidence of GNR parentage was to be had at Havenhouse station. This was the delightful 'right away' received by the driver of the 1439 Boston-Skegness service as he prepared to leave the platform and pass over the level crossing – a welcome that just cannot be replicated by a colour light signal! *Both David Holmes*

4 September

As well as loco-hauled trains disappearing, long trains of any sort became very much rarer. Not so here, however, as slim-line Class 202 'Hastings' DEMUs Nos 1012 and 1016 approach Chiselhurst – on the old SE&CR route to the south – forming the 0915 Charing Cross-Hastings service. Of the 12 cars shown here, just two from set 1012 survive, Driving Car 60016 *Mountfield* and Trailer 60708, both at St Leonard's Railway Engineering. The remainder of the vehicles from set 1012 were cut up between 1989 and 1992, and all six cars from No 1016 were disposed of between 1987 and 1998. *Brian Morrison*

25

▲ 6 September

A natural temptation for a photographer would have been to go in closer and focus on the DMU, but by 'stepping back' and incorporating the debris of the coastline, what looks to be an abandoned building and the attractive sloping contours on either side of the railway, he has given us a far more interesting view. The low sun, too, adds to the mix, by picking out all manner of details, and the whole makes for a very pleasing shot of a Carlisle-Barrow service, near Nethertown, on the Cumbrian Coast line. *Tom Heavyside*

▼ 26 September

SR EMUs spent much of the latter part of the 1980s being shuffled, re-arranged, refurbished and renumbered, to the extent that it became almost impossible to keep up with it all, and for those of us north of the Thames it was totally bewildering! Where whole sets could not be made or maintained, hybrid sets appeared, such as No 7700, seen in Platform 16 at Waterloo, waiting to form the 1028 service to Reading. At this time it was made up of spare VEP and CIG cars Nos 76690 (ex-7840), 62200 (7739), 70798 (7718) and 76639 (7365)! *MJS*

3 October

Here is another Class 50, but by this date notice how short the length of loco-hauled stock is becoming. To the left of the train, supports for Brunel's original viaduct can still be seen, but now wholly reclaimed by nature, as No 50003 *Temeraire* crosses a later version at Coombe St Stephen,

near Liskeard, with the 1128 Plymouth-Penzance train. Once more, placing the train into its landscape has provided an artistic portrait, especially with the results of ploughing beyond, rather than a mere 'record shot'. Introduced to the WCML on 12 January 1968, *Temeraire* ended its days at Laira on 15 July 1991. *Brian Morrison*

▼ 4 October

'Cornish Railways' is the legend on the nose of No 37196 *Tre Pol and Pen* as it approaches Lostwithiel with a Goonbarrow-Carne Point clay-hoods train. Yet again the photographer has made excellent use of available infrastructure; the semaphore – superbly strategically placed – the hoods themselves – now history – the train's position and the direction of the light all combine to make a truly evocative scene. For the photographic enthusiast, the shot was taken on a Nikon FM2 camera, using Ilford XP1 b&w film, rated at 400ASA, and employing a 180mm lens with a shutter speed of 1/500th and aperture at f8! Also, the shot was a 'one off' as it was taken from builder's scaffolding on the outside of a structure being refurbished, during their tea break! *Brian Morrison*

▶ 10 October

We have already mentioned liveries and their development, and the speed of their variation and proliferation notched up a gear from 1985; initially, it was strange to see classes large and small with many permutations among their numbers. The honour of being the very first Class 47 to be regaled in InterCity livery went to No 47487, seen here at Liverpool Street station still newly outshopped, waiting to leave with the 1230 express to Norwich. When first seen, the style did not seem to suit the class, somehow making them look smaller than they were! The new garb did not serve to prolong No 47487's life, as it was withdrawn on 7 December 1988, from Crewe Diesel depot.

On the same day, but slightly further north, we are back to 'yesteryear', as the two '37s' have yet to lose their all-over 'Corporate Blue'. Standing on Gospel Oak station, having arrived from Liverpool Street by way of Broad Street station, I was delighted to capture this view of No 37019 piloting 37038 on a westbound container freight from Ripple Lane. Among the earliest of the class and still bearing its split headcode boxes, No 37019 was introduced in June 1961 and still nominally remained in service 44 years later, although no longer in regular use. No 37038, by contrast, was younger by 11 months and was withdrawn in October 1999. Happily it saw re-introduction and also remained 'on the books' in 2005. *Both MJS*

▲ 16 November

One happy development during the 1980s was the emergence of regular steam runs to Stratford-upon-Avon from the now reprieved Marylebone station. Having overcome the shortsighted and somewhat mischievous political attempt to close the former GCR London terminus, BR did take steps to slowly build up its usage. One of the early – and very popular – locomotives drafted in to haul the steam specials was Bulleid's No 34092 *City of Wells*, and it is seen here accelerating away from High Wycombe station on the outward, morning run. *MJS*

▼ 7 December

Another regular – and equally popular – participant in these specials was one of Gresley's magnificent 'A4s'. Built in 1937 and named *Sir Nigel Gresley* after its designer, it became No 60007 after Nationalisation, but with its original number of 4498, and complete with garter blue livery, it is seen storming the bank out of Saunderton with 'The William Shakespeare' express. Note how the backlit smoke adds to the less usual view. *MJS*

8 December

We have seen Bolton previously with a Sunday engineer's train, and here is another. Once again this photographer has chosen to present a less than normal approach to create his image, and by including such an expanse of the signal box he has been very brave. However, in my view, it works! The bold name, the slightly rotting timbers, finial and cross-town vista all serve to enhance the less than spectacular train hauled by No 97405. During the re-modelling of the station, the disguised Class 40 – formerly No 40060 – is handling a ballast train, presumably ready to assist the workmen at their labours in the platforms behind. Built in February 1960, to replace steam on the WCML prior to electrification, it had been withdrawn in January 1985 from Carlisle (Kingmoor) depot, but was to have a reprieve four months later for engineering work – hence the renumbering to 97405. This use was short-lived, however, with its end coming from Crewe Diesel Depot on 9 March 1987 and cutting by Vic Berry one year later. *Tom Heavyside*

1986

3 January

Framing, again, is important here, as well as the superbly controlled exposure. Many of us could have been to this spot and considered the photographic opportunities, but, I venture to suggest, most would have positioned themselves closer to the edge of the parkland; but by standing back and including a grass foreground and the two trees to frame the train, viaduct and cityscape, the image is much the stronger. With just five short years left before the service was turned over to Light Rail operation, a Class 504 unit crosses Radcliffe Viaduct as the 1245 Bury-Manchester Victoria service. *Tom Heavyside*

▲ 9 January

How many of us, I wonder, would have travelled halfway across a county on a snowy Thursday to take railway photographs in dull weather conditions? Happily, this photographer has done just that and has been rewarded with a long-distant view of double-headed '31s' on an equally long-gone freight service. Watched by the station employee, who has obviously been indulging in a little snow-shovelling, Nos 31156 (in blue) and 31145 (in Railfreight grey livery) head through Melton Mowbray station bound for East Anglia with a stone train from the ARC sidings in Loughborough; like the train, the sidings have long since disappeared. *Horace Gamble*

▶ 4 February

While standardisation is nothing new to railways, the modular approach to the design of the Class 58s was a real departure from tradition. They were supposed to present a pointer to the future of locomotive design, but the results were not successful enough for the concept to be followed when the Class 60s emerged just a few years later. During a period when Doncaster Works (late re-named BRML) was still in the construction business, the cab ends of No 58042, with new-style ventilation grilles, stand in No 4 Bay, awaiting their place on a bodyshell. *Colin Marsden*

33

8 February

This was another wintry weekend and a pleasurably eventful one for your author. On that day, the LNER Society ran one of its famous long-distance specials, taking a Class 50 from Marylebone to Buxton/Manchester Piccadilly and back, and enthusiast delights were many and varied. While awaiting the arrival of the special at High Wycombe, many of the gathered throng turned their attention and cameras to the unusually long service train, as it passed under the Amersham-Wycombe road bridge and slowed for the stop at the staggered up platform, off to the right of this view. August 1957-vintage No 53124 leads the six-coach set over the previous night's snowfall as the 0637 Stratford-upon-Avon to Paddington service.

The sun shone brightly for most of the day, after the cloud and snow of the previous evening and overnight, and this (rare) view is of No 50016 *Barham*, swinging its train away from the Midland main line at Knighton South Junction, to take the line to Burton-on-Trent. Note the accumulations of snow on and around Leicester's Sports Centre, on the left. The train then went on to Derby, where a second '50' took over.

By the time the special reached Buxton, the sun had disappeared, clouds had gathered and the later part of the tour to Manchester Piccadilly and return was accompanied by more snow flurries. To assist access to Buxton's station stop, the train was graced with the provision of No 45022 to haul it into the platform. In the dull, snowy conditions, tour participants detrain to explore the station and the attendant loco shed or to briefly investigate the nearby town. *All MJS*

1986

8 March

This view once seemed so permanent, but is now unrepeatable, for so much has disappeared, with virtually only the office tower block in the centre distance still standing! Once the mainstay of front-line passenger services on the Midland main line, '45s' had been relegated to lesser duties by HSTs some four years prior to this view of No 45108 passing Bell Lane, Leicester, heading towards the city's London Road station with an up parcels working, but perhaps it is the magnificent signal gantry that is more greatly missed. As with so many others in this part of the UK, it was swept away with the new signalling introduced with the closing of the 'Leicester Gap' in 1987. No 45108 also disappeared in 1987, from Tinsley on 4 August. *Horace Gamble*

24 March

Coal traffic changed dramatically in the wake of the miners' strike of 1984/5, with closure of collieries and the introduction of 'merry-go-round' trains and fresh rolling-stock, but stone trains were not exempt. In the days when PGA wagons were common and so often under the control of Class 56s, No 56033 rounds the curve at Clink Road Junction, accelerating towards Westbury and its ultimate destination at Eastleigh, from ARC's Whatley Quarry on the far side of Frome. Note the recess on the right, where the junction signal box had stood until just a year or so prior to this view. *Colin Marsden*

26 March

As with coal and stone, parcels and other freight traffic progressively suffered changing trends and fashions over the two decades from 1980. One high-profile casualty of this was BR's once much-vaunted 'Speedlink' freight service, summarily swept away only a handful of years after this view and against much opposition. In happier times, front-line WCML locomotive No 87007 *City of Manchester*, in InterCity livery, is 'slumming it' by hauling an up 'Speedlink' on the slow lines through Hemel Hempstead at 1145 on this bright spring morning, with an impressive array of vehicles behind it. Introduced in October 1973, '007 remained anonymous until graced with its name at Manchester Piccadilly on 1 November 1977.

A few hours earlier, No 310090 is on the same stretch of track as it enters Hemel Hempstead as the 0937 Birmingham-Euston stopper. Each enthusiast or student of our railways has his/her own favourite, but to my mind one of the most aesthetically pleasing of all EMU designs was the '310s', a class that had obviously received careful design thought and proceeded to give many years of valuable service. Later refurbished and renumbered – to 310105 – to concentrate on work in and around the West Midlands, it was reduced to just three cars in February 1996 until finally withdrawn in June 2001 and stored at Shoeburyness. *Both MJS*

▲ 16 April

The introduction in the UK of Class 59s from 1986 brought about great changes to the Merehead trains and weakened the stranglehold previously held by Class 56s. Previously seen on page 36, No 56033 is still hard at work close to Frome, here heading west with the 1005 Acton-Merehead Quarry empties. Note the three larger hoppers at the front of the train and the wintry feel of the surrounding countryside. *Colin Marsden*

▼ 10 May

In the second half of the decade the Venice-Simplon Orient Express set of Pullman cars toured extensively around the southern half of the country, giving great pleasure and luxury entertainment to many hundreds in the process. During 1986 the VSOE 'Bournemouth Belle' continued to operate and is seen here, complete with a magnificent and appropriate headboard, at West Byfleet, headed by No 33111. The '33s' were once a common sight on former SR metals and are now much missed. Originally D6528, new in October 1960, '111 was one of the small class of 33/1s, originating in 1965, converted for push-pull operation and numbering only 19 examples. The first of this sub-class to be withdrawn was No 33104 in the last month of 1985, and No 33111 followed in June 1991. *Colin Marsden*

▲ 13 May

Way out indeed! Such was the comment from many a railwayman about the 'Quiet Americans' – the Class 59s. Built at General Motors' La Grange workshops in Illinois – and the forerunners of the Class 66s that became ubiquitous throughout the system a decade or so later – they had been shipped aboard a Dutch freighter and they certainly proved to be a revolutionary locomotive in both design and performance and like nothing we had seen before in the UK. They made BR sit up and take notice! Privately owned by Foster Yeoman, for use on its stone trains out of Merehead, they impressed all who saw them. No 59002 – to become *Yeoman Enterprise* some six weeks later at Merehead – heads east through Hungerford station at the head of the 1705 Yeoman train from Merehead, details picked out beautifully in the late afternoon sunshine. It is doubtful that this train will need to heed the 90mph limit sign! *MJS*

▼ 15 May

Another view of a train in its context, this time the glorious south Oxfordshire countryside. Still clinging to routine daily passenger workings, No 50045 *Achilles* glides gracefully northwards past the nonchalantly grazing sheep with the 1700 Paddington-Oxford semi-fast train. Note the length of this relatively short-distance service, although, carrying commuters home from work in London, no doubt the ample provision of seats was fully required and appreciated. The '50' lost its name for two months in 1989 and was withdrawn from Laira depot on 11 December 1990. *MJS*

▲ 16 May

My first introduction to Watford Junction station and, in particular, the suburban platforms and surviving infrastructure seen here, was in 1982, and was described in picture and words on page 52 of Volume 1 of this series, covering 1980-84. That the infrastructure then in place could be swept away within months of me first seeing it both surprised me and reinforced the maxim that we should snap anything and everything around us, as it so often disappears, almost without warning. The subsequent denuding of these platforms – and the clearance of ageing Class 501 EMUs from services – is well evidenced here as newly introduced replacement '313s' stand empty, waiting to become local trains to Euston. Using front-ends to aesthetic effect, there seem to be sad faces on (left to right) Nos 313012, 313005 and 313003! *MJS*

▼ 17 May

This is the 'down side' of BR's modern image, although the circumstances gave the photographer the chance to create a very pleasing image. The ancient-looking lattice post with its semaphore signal certainly looks the part and adds a glamour all its own to the picture, but it is not helping the actual operations here, as it is not working! Instead, a hand-held green flag served to sanction passage over the level crossing. The driver of No 73127 peers from his cab for permission to move his Chipman's weedkilling train forward. Three months short of two years after this view, the loco was transformed to No 73203, to become one of those converted to haul the push-pull 'Gatwick Express' shuttle trains. Note the holes in the windows of Grain Crossing signal box – whether caused by stones or air gun pellets, they are not a positive image for BR in this area! *Brian Morrison*

19 May

The short ex-GWR branch from Slough to Windsor & Eton Central operates its services day-to-day without fuss or much attention in the railway press. The service provision is largely for commuters and tourists, visiting the 'honeypot' town with its castle and other attractions. One of the latter, creating an extra lure for the visitor during the 1980s, was the Queen Victoria Exhibition, simulating the arrival of that monarch at Windsor in the latter years of the 19th century. The boundary boarding of this exhibition can be seen on the left as the 1033 service from Slough arrives. Single-car DMU Class 121 'set' L128 (No 55028) is coupled to Class 121 Driving Trailer L283 (No 54283) to form a standard two-car provision for this single-line branch, drawing to a halt in the glorious early summer sunshine.

Back in Slough shortly afterwards, another 'routine' train roars through the station on its way to Paddington. From 1976 the HSTs gradually assumed the mantle of running the GWR main line expresses and over the succeeding three decades the design has proved its value, in service, reliability and popularity with the travelling public. On this day, in one of the various InterCity livery permutations, power car No 43034 bears the set number 253017 as it speeds towards the metropolis but, with No 43180 at the rear, it proves that the original intention to have permanent sets has not worked. The allocation and marking of '253' (GWML) and '254' (ECML) soon lost their meaning during the 1980s and the practice was abandoned. *Both MJS*

▲ 28 May

We have seen No 37038 before, on page 29, but here the loco is seen alone and further north, on the racetrack of the ECML some 5 miles south of York, hurrying along the slow lines at Colton with a near uniform up 'Speedlink' service in the bright afternoon summer sunshine. Like its classmate in the earlier photograph, it still retains the split headcode boxes and also retains the nose-end doors, fitted when new. Emerging from English Electric's Vulcan Foundry in May 1962 and allocated to Neville Hill depot in Leeds, it remained at that depot until after the end of steam in 1968. *MJS collection*

▼ 28 May

Being a child of the Midland main line, I grew to love the '45s' – after recovering from the antipathy to them for usurping steam traction in and around Leicester! – and one of my own personal favourites was No 45007 (and nothing to do with James Bond!). Towards the end of its life and more than three years since it had itself been replaced on front-line duties by HSTs, the loco stands at the blocks in an unusually light and airy St Pancras, having brought a parcels train into the terminus and awaiting its next trip. It is creditably clean, and unnamed – it was to be unofficially christened *Taliesin* at Tinsley in June 1987, just a month before being withdrawn! *MJS*

28 May

The introduction of the so-called 'second generation' DMUs put paid to the working lives of so many of the then affectionately labelled 'Heritage' units, and these suddenly became much more loved than they had ever been during their earlier lifetimes. As is the way of things, the new replacements did not enjoy the devotion of enthusiasts – and it has to be said that many of them did fall short of what had gone before. An example was Class 142 from Leyland/BREL Derby, effectively a bus body on rail bogies. The resultant hybrid was not a universal success with either

the public or railway authorities: the ride was rough compared to what passengers had been used to – and progress surely should bring improvement! – and reliability was not good. They plied their trade along branches and non-main-line routes, attempting to reduce costs in a way similar to their forebears. New to this line and known as 'Pacers', a typical duty is as seen here, with the new driver of No 142028 – new in August 1985 – about to take the single-line token as the unit leaves Rufford station as the 1804 Ormskirk-Preston stopper. *Tom Heavyside*

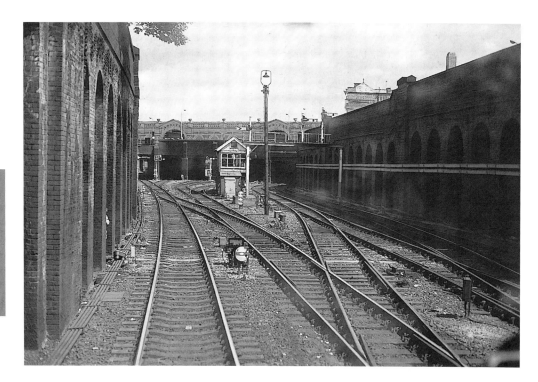

28 May

On this day I was privileged to join Jeremy English in the cab of a Midland main line HST, as he filmed the run from St Pancras to Sheffield for his 'Railscene' series of videos. Having been born and bred in Leicester, I knew a good 50% of the route quite well and was able, therefore, to contribute to the in-cab conversation with some knowledge, but the real bonus for me was seeing familiar surroundings and landmarks from a whole new perspective. For example, I had seen the southern approach to Leicester's London Road station from above, but to witness the cutting on the ground was totally different. Here, Leicester South signal box is still in operation, but only for another year, as the 1100 service from St Pancras slows for the station stop.

Fifteen or so miles north of Leicester is Loughborough's Midland station, where I began my long railway career as a spotter, on my way home from Loughborough College School in 1955. Sadly, the railway changed substantially over the succeeding 30 years, both on the ground to the left and in the fortunes of Brush Engineering, on the right. Here, again viewed from the cab of the HST, the signal box immediately to the north of the station is still functional, but, like its counterpart in Leicester, was demolished after the closure of the 'Leicester Gap' in 1987. *Both MJS*

1986

5 June
Originally built for the lines out of St Pancras and the services to Bedford, Class 127 DMUs were ousted from these duties in the 1980s, replaced by electric traction that henceforth became known as 'Bed-Pan' units! Many were withdrawn from service – and most cut at Vic Berry's yard – but some survived for further usage in the North West as Express Parcels units, by the removal of seats and the fitting of roller-shutter blinds midway along the carriage. Here unit 916,

comprising Nos 55976 (ex-51625) and 55986 (ex-51627), both converted in June 1985 and re-liveried in dark blue with a red stripe, with two vans in tow, runs between Bolton and Lostock Junction as a Manchester-Preston duty. Happily, at the end of this life, both units were preserved, No 51625 at the Midland Railway Centre in October 1990 and No 51627 to Crewe Heritage Centre in August 1992. *Tom Heavyside*

▲ 9 June

As mentioned before, the '45s' were ousted from front-line duties on the Midland main line, and in many instances this meant that they were used on a greater volume of secondary routes and duties, many being cross-country. For some years they were regular performers on east-west passenger turns in the northern half of the UK, and one member of the class is seen here passing Colton with a Newcastle-Llandudno service. No 45115, new in December 1960, is here un-named but was unofficially christened *Apollo* at Tinsley on 3 September 1987, just nine months before withdrawal on 13 June 1988, from that same depot. *MJS collection*

▼ 25 June

The GW150 celebrations were meant to be a magnificent 'party' to recognise the longevity of 'God's Wonderful Railway', its past contribution to our country's heritage, and the remaining elements of that contribution. The announcement of the closure of Swindon Works at the same time, however, put a massive dampener on proceedings and certainly left a nasty taste in mouths throughout the UK, not just among the very angry burghers of Swindon itself. One of the last items through the Works, having received attention and some refurbishment, was 'Thumper' No 205009, seen here standing alongside the GW main line outside part of the Works complex. Happily, the buildings in the background survived to carry on workshop duties under private hands, and while the wall behind the 'Thumper' still stands into the 21st century, that is all it is. Used in 1990 for the brief 'NRM of the south' exhibition, the building's roof and 'innards' were stripped shortly afterwards, and a car park opened in the resultant space. *MJS*

28 June

Whichever way you view it, York station is a magnificent structure, visually appealing in its grandeur and a wonderful example of the pride, confidence and vision of the Victorian railway champions. Compare this with modern constructions and it is easy to see what has been cast aside. Another west-east cross-country service rests briefly in the main down platform, as No 45040 – once named *The King's Shropshire Light Infantry* – prepares to leave the Liverpool-Scarborough working that it has brought across the Pennines, with No 47488 waiting alongside to take over for the final stretch to the coast. Initially withdrawn in July 1987, No 45040 was re-introduced on 23 October of that year, to be converted for Departmental use as No 97412. In that guise it was withdrawn on 2 August 1988.

Slightly later in the day, York is now the destination rather than the venue. Another unit type that usurped its 'Heritage' predecessors, but was also poor by comparison, was yet another Leyland/BREL Derby 'invention', the Class 141. Introduced between October 1983 and October 1984, initially as '141/0s', they were all renumbered as '141/1s' five years later when their couplings were changed for compatibility purposes. Here, an unidentified original-style unit shows off its similarity to the road bus on the right, with its narrow-looking straight body and somewhat questionable construction – which, with poor-riding bogies, gave a very unstable and uncomfortable journey experience for passengers. As it enters Poppleton station as the 1528 Leeds-York local service, the driver prepares to hand over the single-line token. Note how the photographer has successfully handled the 'contra-jour' lighting to retain detail in the front of the unit. *Both Tom Heavyside*

1 July
A balding head looks back along the train as No 31440 backs its stock into the platform at Liverpool Lime Street station, the western end of the east-west cross-country services already seen. Here we have another example of Victorian vision and ideas of grandeur, although on this occasion the overall trainshed is not quite as magnificent in scale as that at York. The train will form the 1245 to Sheffield. New as D5628 in June 1960, the loco's first TOPS number was 31204, but this then became 31440 on 18 April 1984, when it became a further addition to the existing '31/4' sub-class. Although outwardly in fine condition in this portrait, it only had a further nine months of life left, being withdrawn from Immingham on 5 March 1987 and cut up at Vic Berry's Leicester yard exactly one year later. *Tom Heavyside*

9 July

Once again we have an example of this photographer's penchant for putting the train within its (often natural) surroundings. He often seeks to add extra items of interest to the composition, and here he has cleverly introduced the magnificent castle in the background, balanced by the admittedly more diminutive house to the right of the train. No 47633 is seen soon after leaving Pitlochry, forming the 1630 Inverness-Glasgow express. The large body-side numerals were a boon to spotters and, with BR's full-size double-arrow logo and wrap-around yellow ends, made for a not unpleasing livery for the '47's'. Originally new as D1668 in March 1965 – as *Orion*, one of a batch of named engines allocated to BR(WR) – TOPS converted it to No 47083 exactly nine years after introduction. Sadly, the name was lost in December 1985, concurrent with the conversion to 47633. Withdrawal came at Eastfield depot on 26 April 1991. *Tom Heavyside*

▼ **24 August**

Another example of the value of placing the train within its context, this time from a different photographer: not overly concentrating on the actual train, but including a fair degree of background countryside, has given both the subject matter and the overall composition 'room to breathe'. The shallow foreground counterpointing with the proliferation of trees beyond has given an added bonus that enhances the finished product. Aller Junction is more often seen looking north, but is here viewed in the direction of Plymouth, as No 47639 approaches with the 1225 Penzance-Liverpool Lime Street holiday season service. Note the newly installed colour-light signal on the right, and the unusually long 12-coach train! Another BR(WR) locomotive, new in 1965 as D1648, it ran without a name. Becoming No 47064 in 1974 and 47639 on 24 February 1986, it became *Industry Year 1986* at Euston on 9 June. The cast nameplate is plainly visible here, but it only remained fixed until October 1988! On 9 February 1990 its number changed again, to 47851, in which guise it was given the name *Traction Magazine* at Derby on 15 January 2002. *Colin Marsden*

▶ **20 September**

We have already seen the introduction of the Class 58s, built exclusively for freight operations. They were very rarely seen on passenger duties in our period of review, but this scene shows one enjoying the limelight prior to officiating on the very first '58'-hauled passenger service out of King's Cross. Standing at the terminus, No 58039, complete with *Rugeley Power Station* nameplate, received just seven days earlier, is the recipient of much attention before getting under way as the 'Lincolnshire Coast Pullman', bound for Cleethorpes and Skegness. Just six months old at this time, it was withdrawn from Toton in December 1999, a victim of changing traffic patterns, the introduction of newer locomotives and economic perceptions – a criminal waste of resources and taxpayers' money. Its last overhaul had been at Doncaster on 30 May 1997 and it had only run a paltry 4,994 hours from then to withdrawal. *Colin Marsden*

▶ **11 October**

One legacy of the 'Railway Mania' of the latter half of the 19th century was the bewildering and impressive array of station layouts and architectural designs. Much of it was, of course, dictated by the situation 'on the ground' as well as railway politics and, sadly, much has been dispensed with over the years, following yet more trends, ideas, economics and, yes, 'progress', but even in the 1980s it was possible to find delight and character, such as here at Ulverston, on the former Furness Railway route from Barrow to Carnforth. Highly unusual, with the single line between platforms, it provides a superb backdrop to Class 108 DMU Driving Trailer No 54262 as it leads Driving Motor 53955 into the station, forming the 1345 Lancaster-Carlisle service (despite the destination blind!). *Tom Heavyside*

6 November

South Wales has seen as much transformation in its railways as anywhere in the country, with the Valleys being particularly hard hit, but much of that change has been missed by railway photographers. Those who have braved the trip to record matters, however, have come away with interesting and often poignant views. Treherbert used to be at the head of a Valley 'web' of lines spreading south-west and south-east, and north-east to Aberdare through a long tunnel. The latter was lost completely in 1966 and the south-west route to Bridgend closed to passengers on 15 July 1970, and completely in December of that year. However, the former Taff Vale route to Cardiff and beyond remains, partly as single track, and that stretch is seen here, near Ystrad Rhondda, as No

W51132 of Cardiff Class 116 set C331 leads a Treherbert-Penarth train.

The second view again shows a train with an interesting backdrop, this time fascinating with the folds and plateaux, presumably a legacy of past mining operations. The early afternoon sun makes very attractive shadows as DMU set C304 arrives at Ton Pentre station, on the former Taff Vale Railway, as the 1350 Penarth-Treherbert service – the reverse direction to that seen above. Six weeks earlier, on 29 September, the station had been renamed from Ystrad Rhondda in preparation for the introduction of a timetabled half-hourly service, but the obvious track rationalisation and architectural rebuilding has destroyed the station's previous inherent aesthetic qualities. *Both Tom Heavyside*

8 November

Yet again, this photographer shows how to craft a pleasing image by utilising available 'props': the church in the background, amidst its village and atop the hill; the sweeping slopes on either side of the railway; the train in exactly the correct position; and last, but certainly not least, the open gateway. As any member of a camera club will know, judges hate a closed gate in the foreground,

seeing it as a barrier to the eye and causing the viewer to climb a virtual obstacle before being able to appreciate the picture. Pre-'Sprinterisation', the Cardiff-Portsmouth route was often graced with Class 33s on passenger services, and here No 33027 *Earl Mountbatten of Burma* is framed by trees and hedgerows as it passes Bathampton on its run south. It lost its name in August 1989 and was withdrawn from Eastleigh on 5 July 1991. *Tom Heavyside*

1986

28 December

There have been numerous published photographs of the infamous pile of loco bodies at Vic Berry's scrapyard in Leicester, but relatively few of other aspects of the scrapping business. As well as piles of coaches and box vans at various times, there was the usual detritus of items not completely finished with, but discarded until their time came. In these last days of 1986, cabs from Class 40s, 45s and 25s – including that of No 25284 – lie in no particular order alongside the Great Central Way, built on the trackbed of the old GCR main line. Note the somewhat flimsy fencing distinguishing yard from footpath! Into the 21st century, the site has been transformed, with housing occupying the whole of the foreground area and the extensive road overbridge served with sentence of death. *MJS*

18 February

The introduction of the Class 59s at the end of the decade truly transformed the Foster Yeoman stone trains, with their ability to haul prodigious loads unassisted, both pleasing their owners and amazing many within and outside BR. Prior to their introduction double-heading was common, as seen here. Moving away from the GW main line, No 37001 (the second oldest of the class and adorned with Stratford's 'Cockney Sparrow' motif) and classmate 37040 climb the bank from Acton Poplar Junction to Acton Wells with the 0905 Acton-Purfleet freight. New on 12 December 1960, '001 was converted by additional ballast on 4 December 1987 (to increase tractive effort) and given the number 37707. In contrast, '040, new to Neville Hill in June 1962 as D6740, remained unaltered throughout its life. Both nominally survived into the 21st century. *Colin Marsden*

19 February

Not quite as graceful or majestic as those already seen at York and Liverpool Lime Street, the extensive trainshed at Southport is still impressive. Twin DMU cars Nos 54439 and 54533 emerge from the shadows into the early afternoon winter sunshine as the 1215 service to Manchester Victoria, with the driver obviously feeling the cold and wearing his storm coat! Originally No 56439, lead car 54439 was a Cravens Class 105 DTCL of October 1958, and is very close to the end of its useful life in this view, being withdrawn eight months later and cut at Mayer Newman's Snailwell scrapyard in November 1987. EMUs Nos 507015 and 508132 are on the left. *Tom Heavyside*

25 February

We have already commented on the introduction of 'second generation DMUs' and the somewhat retrograde step with the inadequacies of units such as the Class 141s. Here we have two more views, this time of set No 141119. The very basic design of the unit – arguably a backward step from previous years – is matched by the state of Knottingley station, with its rudimentary wooden platform, fencing and waiting shelter and the obvious abandonment of an earlier platform face on the left. A handful of travellers are about to 'enjoy' their journey as they board the rear car of the 1104 Leeds-Goole service.

Later in the day, the same set returns along the former L&YR route, this time with No 55539 leading as it restarts from the Hensall stop, just two stations from its destination at Goole. Originally constructed by Leyland/BREL Derby as No 141018 in June 1984, renumbering to 141119 came in August 1988. Note the 'L&YR' legend still remaining on the doorway of 'Station House' and the same company's warning sign on the house wall. Note also the steps to assist boarding the train from the low-level platform, the slightly intricate fencing in the foreground, protecting the roadway and giving access to the platform, and the coal train retreating into the distance. *Both Tom Heavyside*

10 March

In the mid-1980s some Class 45s were fitted with a headlight, with a view to their being retained into the 1990s. This policy was short-lived, however, and hardly had the first fittings begun than the class was facing extinction. One of their last 'first link' duties was the Trans-Pennine route, connecting the North East with the North West. Here No 45137 (now devoid of its *The Bedfordshire and Hertfordshire Regiment (TA)* nameplates) looks healthy enough as it accelerates out of Manchester Victoria at the head of the 0820 Newcastle-Liverpool service. Sadly, the end was not far away, with withdrawal from Tinsley on 15 June. Note the on-track plant temporarily stabled in the background.

Those machines are again seen here, slightly later in the day, as No 25191 approaches Victoria with a short, empty engineer's train. The 'Rat' has even less time to enjoy revenue-earning service, being withdrawn just eight days later, together with all the remaining few examples of the class – at a stroke, they were extinct on BR. Introduced on 29 March 1965, as D7541 and allocated to Toton, it remained a Midland loco until just prior to the end of steam, when, in May 1968, it was transferred to the West Coast Main Line. Acquiring its TOPS number in April 1974, its final home was Crewe Diesel Depot. *Both MJS*

► 12 March

Nottingham Midland station has seen many changes over the years and a few shifts of favour, with the varying fortunes of and plans for the Midland main line as well as the 'branch' through Trowell Junction. Despite demographic changes, however, it has retained a through service to London into the 21st century – even on a Sunday – and this looks secure for the foreseeable future. The Trowell route has been saved; Mansfield has again been joined to the city with the re-instatement of a once-abandoned line; and the city now boasts one of the most successful light rail systems in the country. Again captured during an escape from a Ten-Pin Bowling tour, HST power car No 43122 waits in Platform 5b with doors wide

open ready for impending travellers, before acting as trailer car on the 1150 express service to St Pancras. *MJS*

▼ 19 March

Here is another example where assiduous use of even spindly, stark, late-winter tree branches has served to enhance the image and transform what would otherwise have been a very ordinary picture. Roughly midway between Reading and

Newbury and close to the position of once-important water troughs, No 50023 *Howe* speeds westwards with the 1145 Paddington-Penzance express, a pleasant sight of a loco and coaches – albeit a real mixed bunch in place of the more standard HST set! Not yet 20 years old and certainly not worn out, *Howe*, introduced in May 1968, was withdrawn from Laira on 15 October 1990. Sadly, it was not one to see preservation. *Colin Marsden*

28 March

Another typical 'trademark' view from this photographer and another loco-hauled train, this time with a healthy cons st of 11 coaches – again of mixed styles and liveries. Kearsley station, serving the community seen in the distance, on the former L&YR route between Manchester Victoria and Bolton, is left behind on the far right as No 47490 heads north-west with a Harwich-Glasgow long-distance cross-country working. Pylons and chimneys old and new dominate the background,

contrasting with the softer presence of trees and river. No 47490 was another engine to have several incarnations: built at Brush in March 1964 as D1725, it gained its TOPS number in February 1974. It remained unnamed until 23 September 1988, when it became *Bristol Bath Road*, to honour the former GWR steam shed and BR diesel depot. This was replaced by *Resonant* in March 1993 at Crewe Diesel Depot, following which it was renumbered to 47768 on 4 March 1994. *Tom Heavyside*

19 April

A popular venue for photographers as well as holidaymakers, and seen here from a slightly unusual vantage point, the seafront at Dawlish remained little changed throughout the 20th century and has, consequently, become known and loved by countless thousands of visitors over the years. The motive power using the shore-hugging line, however, has changed dramatically and continues to do so to this day. 'Pacer' units, known as 'Skippers' in Devon and Cornwall, did not survive long in the South West, as their tyre wear was excessive compared to conventional DMUs. During its short stay, No 142025, new in December 1985, heads away from its Dawlish station stop as the 1440 Exeter-Paignton local. Note the gentle waves breaking lazily on the beach, although the absence of bathers indicates that it is probably too chilly for stripping off! *Colin Marsden*

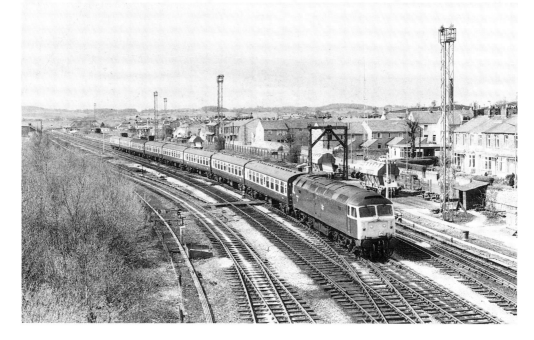

21 April

As the spread of 'unitisation' gathered pace throughout the UK, the popularity of loco-hauled trains grew in proportion to their disappearance. Route after route saw hordes of devotees flocking to take advantage of the trains while they were still available, not least on cross-country services, along the North Wales coast and the scenic Settle-Carlisle line. Although most would probably regard Hellifield as being the southern entrance to the S&C, Skipton, only a few miles closer to Leeds, could equally claim the honour, although, as seen here, the railway's surroundings are nowhere near as picturesque as out on the moors! No 47488 approaches the town from the north with the eight-coach 1040 Carlisle-Leeds service, at a time when, although reprieved from immediate sentence of death, it was by no means certain that the route, linking Yorkshire with Cumbria, would survive and thrive.

Ilkley once had a link to Skipton provided by the Midland Railway on its route to Scotland, but this was axed in July 1965 – together with the old Otley & Ilkley Railway spur from Burley to Arthington, leaving just the ex-O&IR terminus station to accommodate trains to Leeds and beyond, over the MR route south-east from Burley. On a dull spring day, a small group wait to board the 1640 service to Leeds and Hull, formed of the classic Class 101 units Nos E51210 and 54398. The former was built by Metropolitan Cammell in September 1958 and remained with its original number throughout, while No 54398 saw life as 56398 in June 1958, succumbed to withdrawal in March 1989 and was immediately cut up by Vic Berry. Note how the glass has been removed from the central trainshed arch. *Both Tom Heavyside*

▲ **21 April**

A telephoto lens can be a real asset for a railway photographer, giving the potential for interesting slants on traditional locations and images, especially with a slightly distorted or truncated perspective. The use of one here, together with the nerve to point into the sun while retaining detail in the 'shadow' areas, has placed 'Pacer' No 142023 – new in December 1985 – exactly on the 'golden third' amid the lines at Aller Junction, as it forms an empty stock working from Paignton to Exeter, past the confident-looking signal box. *Colin Marsden*

▼ **23 April**

Once more we have examples of railway architecture – not the grandiose arching trainsheds already witnessed, but a more subtle yet still stylish design. However, this view also evidences the importance of serendipity, for just months after I escaped from yet another Barclays Bank Ten-Pin Bowling tour to visit Portsmouth & Southsea station, to capture this view, the deteriorating wooden canopy seen above the train and to the right was swept away, to be replaced by a more modern affair. No 7347 is the trailing unit here of the 1506 Portsmouth Harbour-Waterloo semi-fast service. *MJS*

▲ 25 April

Here is a delightfully attractive scene, despite being made up of disparate parts that on their own do not stand out. The direction of light, the semaphore gantry – with the 'peg' half down – the squat signal box, the shining rails and the rising left-to-right gradient throughout the image all combine to create a winner. Derby Works Class 108 DMBS 53607, new in June 1958 as 50607, arrives at Scarborough at the head of the 1033 service from Hull. Withdrawn in March 1990, it was another of the DMU family cut up by Vic Berry, this time five months after withdrawal. Note the two different cars behind, making a distinctly mixed rake. *Tom Heavyside*

▼ 27 April

Severn Tunnel Junction, both the station and the surrounding sidings, is but a shadow of its former self, and the decline in the site's importance continued during the 1980s. Concurrently, BR's 'Speedlink' wagonload freight service suffered changes in traffic and fortune, to the effect that it ceased to operate after 8 July 1991. The combination of these two factors gives added poignancy to this view of No 47142 passing through the Wylye Valley at Little Langford as the 1605 Eastleigh-Severn Tunnel Junction 'Speedlink' train. The May 1964-vintage '47' lasted slightly longer, being honoured with *The Sapper* name at Long Marston on 3 October 1987, then, unofficially, *Traction* at Tinsley on 26 November 1994, before succumbing to the economists at Crewe Diesel Depot on 28 April 1998. *Brian Morrison*

16 May

At the risk of repetition, this is yet another example of using the available surroundings to 'make a silk purse out of a sow's ear'! Taken with his Nikon FM camera and 50mm lens on Ilford FP4 film, shutter speed 1/500th second and aperture f5, the two Class 108 twin-car DMUs forming the 1744 Lancaster-Barrow local pass the site of the old Hest Bank station; but what makes the picture are the housing backdrop, weather-beaten house (old level crossing keeper's cottage?), the empty washing line, white fencing and, above all, the outside privy! *Tom Heavyside*

1987

20 May
Another glimpse of a routine service that has long gone and become more interesting with the passage of time: just months after this view, the 'Severn-Solent' Portsmouth-Cardiff service was handed over to 'Sprinters', obviating the need for a loco change at Bristol, as seen here. However, although saving that operation, the provision of a two-car DMU set was no substitute for even a short length of 'proper' coaches. Here, the driver of No 33207 looks less than happy – at his past or future? – as he abandons his charge at Bristol (Temple Meads), having backed it on to stock for the onward run to Portsmouth Harbour at 1305. One of the 'slim-line' Class 33/2s introduced for operating on the restricted gauge in tunnels on the Tonbridge to Hastings route, No 33207 was

built in March 1962 and honoured with *Earl Mountbatten of Burma* plates in September 1989. Initially withdrawn from Stewart's Lane on 13 February 1997, it was re-instated on 16 July 1999 and was still nominally active in 2005.

One more view of Swindon Works in its death throes: with the local community still smarting from the unfeeling and indecent haste of the decision to close the Works the previous year, some of the very last locos on site – sold to Vic Berry for scrap – wait alongside the Gloucester line before being moved north to Leicester and their fate. Nos 25027 and 25075 stand at the head of the line, with others of the class behind, and also Class 40s in tow. Shortly afterwards the trackwork here was severely rationalised, but the buildings seen behind were given a reprieve, to exist in differing uses. *Both MJS*

▲ 30 May

Looking like some huge railway caterpillar, this, in 1987, was among the 'shapes to come'. With a progressive reduction in rolling-stock requirements, especially from the reduction in loco-hauled trains and greater standardisation, wide variety inexorably became a thing of the past. First-generation 'Sprinters' and EMUs shared a pedigree – often one being an electric version of the other – and the ugly placing of corridor connections on front-ends is well evidenced in this picture of Class 455/7 EMU No 5709, framed by station structures as it leaves Clapham Junction as the 1720 Waterloo-Dorking commuter service. Originally constructed as a three-car set, it inherited 'TS' coach No 71532 in May 1984 from No 508007 when the latter unit moved north to Merseyside. *Brian Morrison*

▼ 20 June

Another Class 45 on cross-country passenger duties, but this time an unidentified service, No 45128 breasts the bank into Leeds station, heading north in early afternoon sunshine, prior to the scene being totally transformed with both electrification and the massive re-organisation and rebuilding in the area in the early years of the 21st century. New as D113 from Crewe on 14 August 1961, its first allocation was to Derby (17A). Thereafter it stayed on the Midland main line until November 1965, when it spent a month on the ER at Sheffield Darnall (41A) before returning home. Thenceforth a Midland loco for most of its life, especially until the take-over of first-link duties by the HSTs in the early 1980s, it finally gravitated to Tinsley depot, in common with most of its siblings. Unofficially named *Centaur* at that depot a month after this picture, it was withdrawn on 2 August 1988, re-instated on 20 February 1989, then dispensed with again on 22 April of that year. *Tom Heavyside*

1987

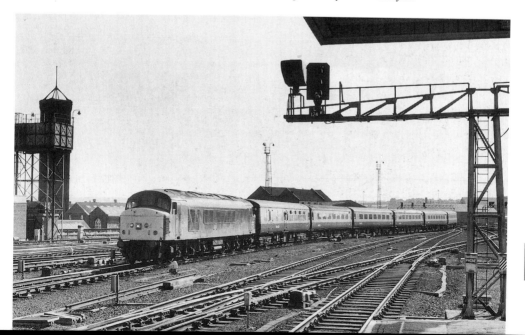

3 July

The railways south of the Thames, especially the closer you come to the metropolis, are often a scene of regular services and constant bustle, not least in the morning and evening rush hours. Thankfully, the mill ons that have been spent in the region over the last 40 years or so have been dedicated more to improving stock and services than sweeping away ancient infrastructure. Consequently there were still delightful views to be had such as this at Guildford, where the ancient canopies, seats and bike-rack all add their own charm to the photograph of three units plying their trade. Left to right, they are Class 412/3 4BEP No 2301 leading the 1355 Waterloo-Portsmouth Harbour service, Class 423 4VEP No 7779 at the rear of the 1430 Guildford-Waterloo, and sister 4VEP No 7824 as the 'slow' 1318 Waterloo-Portsmouth Harbour service. All three unit sets were subsequently renumbered – 2301 to 2311 from September 2002, 7779 to 3079 from August 1987, and 7824 to 3124 from March 1988. *Brian Morrison*

▲ 5 July

As if any proof were necessary, this delightful portrait shows that you do not always need open, rolling countryside, or trees, mountains, historic buildings or atmosphere to create a winning image. Admittedly, good lighting and even sunshine helps, but here it is the combination and juxtaposition of the dock cranes, two empty spoil wagons, industrial buildings, the diminutive diesel shunter and railman that grab and hold the attention. The latter prepares to 'climb aboard' the front steps of Class 03 No 03170 as it moves forward with a single wagon at Birkenhead Docks. One of 230 diesel-mechanical 0-6-0 shunters built jointly by Swindon and Doncaster Works, D2170 entered BR's 'brave new world' on 21 November 1960, initially at Neville Hill steam shed. Sojourns at Selby and Hull (Dairycoates) followed before a return to Leeds in November 1968. A subsequent move to Birkenhead followed, from where the end came on 23 May 1989, as one of the very last of the class to survive. Thankfully, preservation beckoned. *Tom Heavyside*

▼ 29 July

Despite my comments above, brooding mountainsides *do* create atmosphere! With some of the magnificent rugged Scottish scenery readily apparent, No 37413 – now bearing the *Loch Eil Outward Bound* nameplates removed from No 37111 – heads the 0950 Glasgow-Fort William train up the gradient to Tyndrum Summit. The '37s' have seen much re-organising, rebuilding and restructuring since the 1980s, and renumberings to boot! No 37413, built as D6976 in April 1965 as one of a batch sent to Cardiff Canton shed, was originally 37276 from 1974, assuming its new persona on 4 October 1985 when fitted with ETH for passenger work in the Scottish Highlands. A new name was affixed at Bo'ness on 30 September 1997 – *The Scottish Railway Preservation Society* – but by 2005, although still nominally on the rolling-stock register, it was in store, the nameplates having been transferred to No 37411. *Tom Heavyside*

▼ 2 August

Trainspotters – and even slightly more casual enthusiasts – will instantly recognise the appeal portrayed here. Lineside vantage points are popular wherever they provide a clear view of the operations, as here at Crewe as No 86423 passes the Crewe Heritage Centre with a passenger service bound for Euston. Whether car parks, as at Rugby, bridges, level crossings or even station platforms, they are ideal places to savour the very unique appeal of our railway system. Initially E3152 on 7 May 1966, TOPS renumbered it to 86023 in December 1973. This was changed to 86323 on 23 August 1980, then 86423 on 12 November 1986 – then, incredibly, 86623 on 7 October 1990! The loco entered the early years of the 21st century in store in Crewe Basford Hall yard. *Tom Heavyside*

▶ 16 August

Birmingham Railway Carriage & Wagon turned out D5396 in June 1962, whence it travelled south for allocation to Cricklewood (14A). Initially confined to the Midland main line metals, the vast majority of its life was, however, spent in Scotland, moving there in July 1968, to Eastfield depot in Glasgow. Becoming No 27108 under the TOPS system in April 1974 – then 27052 ten years later – it was withdrawn in early July 1987, being one of the last of the class to survive. Its final move, in common with other classmates, was back south, to Vic Berry's Leicester yard. Initially this was for asbestos removal, as there was talk of preservation, but the loco failed to find a buyer and was eventually cut. In fine external condition, it is seen in Berry's yard in this in-between period, complete with bodyside 'Scottie' and appearing to be working a push-pull service! *MJS*

▶ 22 August

The very rare sight of a 'Princess Royal' at Kemble! As the 1980s progressed, more routes were re-opened to steam, and one such was that between Swindon and Gloucester. While less frequent than the outings on, say, the Settle & Carlisle, Cumbrian Coast or between Marylebone and Stratford, who would argue at frequency when quality such as No 6201

Princess Elizabeth was on display. In typical railtour fashion, the day had started out bright and sunny, but by the time the special reached Kemble the clouds had moved across the sun and the weather was closing in! However, this did not stop the obvious excitement and enjoyment of both tour participants and local onlookers – note the number crowding the footbridge! *MJS*

▼ **31 August**

Among the proliferation of both DMUs and EMUs, there were the odd units that were less common. One such was the DEMU Class 210, introduced in 1981 from BREL Derby; they were more experimental than anything else. Only two sets were built, '001' with four cars and '002' with three. In December 1988 two carriages from '001' and one from '002' were converted for Departmental use and the rest then converted to EMU operation, helping towards the development of the Class 317 EMUs. Rarely seen on ordinary services, No 210002 was, therefore, an unusual and very pleasing sight at Newbury – especially as it was the only one still active at the time – at 1550 on this bright sunny afternoon. *MJS*

▼ **31 August**

Once an everyday part of the scene on the lines out of Waterloo, the sight of Class 50s on Salisbury/Exeter trains became very much harder to capture as the end of the decade approached. The view enhanced by the use of a telephoto lens, No 50008 *Thunderer* accelerates out of Waterloo, near Vauxhall, with the 1210 Exeter St David's train, chasing and overtaking Class 455/7 No 5732 leading the eight-car 1206 Waterloo-Chessington service. New in March 1968 as D408 on the WCML, and becoming No 50008 under TOPS, *Thunderer* gained its name at Laira depot on 1 September 1978. Final withdrawal was at that same depot – then stored as unserviceable – on 5 June 1992. *Brian Morrison*

▲ 7 September

The chalk downs running across the country south of the M4 have a number of carved figures prominent on the hillsides. Many are horses, but the only 'genuine' one is that at Uffington, now thought to be around 3,500 years old. The one seen on the hillside in the background here is much more recent, but still provides a point of interest for the area. Much younger still is No 33118, seen leaving Westbury and heading westwards on the approach to Fairwood Junction with a rake of empty ballast wagons. The 1961-vintage Class 33 remained unnamed throughout its life, which lasted until withdrawal from Eastleigh on 16 April 1993, with cutting being handled at the depot by the close of February 1997. *Tom Heavyside*

▼ 7 September

On the same day that Tom Heavyside was on the former GWR line outside Westbury, Brian Morrison was also on ex-Brunel metals, this time at Old Oak Common, perfectly capturing the juxtaposition of two Class 50s. No 50008 *Thunderer*, seen on page 73, is again hard at work, but this time on slightly more local work than the week before, leaving the capital with the 1612 Paddington-Oxford semi-fast service. Travelling in the opposite direction, Network SouthEast-liveried No 50002 *Superb* approaches with empty stock for Paddington, for use in a later service. Admittedly exaggerated by the positioning of the two locomotives, note how much more powerful *Thunderer* looks in its 'large logo' livery, compared to the NSE styling on *Superb*. *Brian Morrison*

▲ 8 September

The day after his visit to Fairwood Junction, Tom Heavyside is still in the area, but this time a little further south. At Clink Road Junction, with the line to Frome sweeping away right in the distance, No 56048 heads towards Westbury with a stone train from Merehead bound for the metropolis. Another example of a class suited to the 'large logo' livery, the Class 56s were both successful and reliable on their 'heavy freight' duties, before being ousted by new types from North America. Sadly, No 56048 was not permitted to fully justify its investment by these intruders and changing traffic patterns, being out of work early in the 21st century, little more than 20 years after its birth in September 1978. *Tom Heavyside*

▼ 18 September

Another junction joining a main line, this time the venue is Clay Cross, in the industrial heartland of north Derbyshire/ south Yorkshire. Surely one of the most photographed trains of our period – not least due to its being double-headed by the ever-popular Class 37s – was the Lackenby-Corby 'Steel-liner' service. On this day the power is provided by identical 'Railfreight'-liveried Nos 37518 and 37514. The former Nos 37076 and 37115 respectively, the former was new in October 1962 (to the purpose-built diesel depot at Thornaby), was converted and renumbered just two months before this shot, on 9 June 1987, and worked in and around the North East the whole of its life. By comparison, No 37115 was new on 22 February 1963 as D6815 and was allocated to Sheffield Darnall (41A), from where it occasionally worked the former GCR route through Leicester to Banbury and Oxford. Its conversion to 37514 came on 11 March 1987 and it then underwent further change, to become 37609 on 20 April 1995. In this guise it was working from Carlisle Kingmoor depot into 2005. *Colin Marsden*

▲ 22 September

Even modern buildings can add to the overall image. Old Trafford football ground provides a rather more tasteful design as backdrop than some others, and certainly enhances this view of No 31457 heading east with a Liverpool Lime Street-Sheffield service. The loco does look somewhat drab in all-over blue, and four coaches is not particularly spacious accommodation for this service, but it is still preferable to the 'unitised' facilities that came later. Originally from Brush as D5587 in February 1960, to 34B Hornsey depot, it was widely travelled throughout the ER in its first decade. Having become No 31169 under TOPS, conversion for continuing passenger work and renumbering to 31457 came on 22 November 1984. Withdrawal was from Bescot on 11 February 1994. *Tom Heavyside*

▼ 26 September

Another celebrated sight during our period was the infamous 'pile' at Vic Berry's scrapyard. At its height (if you will excuse the pun) there were in the region of 40 loco bodies stacked up, mostly Classes 25 and 27, although Classes 45 and 20 shared the limelight for a while. Bogies were separated and returned to BR for re-use, leaving the bodies for scrapping. Here the mobile crane adds to the general activity, as its powerful magnet is activated to lift some of the discarded components. Nos 25285, 25042 and 25089 await their fates, together with their companions. These three had all gone within a month, but several bodies, closer to the centre of the pile, lasted far longer. *MJS*

▲ 17 October

In contrast to many of the sites we have featured in this volume, Windermere, the terminus of the former LNWR branch from Oxenholme, was left very much out of the limelight by railway photographers. The removal of any meaningful items of platform furniture, however, did not help the cause, but nevertheless the station does retain some of its charm, despite being totally open and only having one platform face. Here, another short-lived exponent of branch-line salvation stands at the buffers, as No 142017, in chocolate-and-cream livery, waits to set off as the 1505 service to Oxenholme. Booths Supermarket, in the background, now stands on the site of the original station building. *Tom Heavyside*

▼ 23 October

Built primarily for coal traffic in the Midlands and that to coal-fired power stations north of the Thames, Class 58s had begun to spread their wings by the second half of the 1980s. In this view, work-stained No 58022 hauls one of the very first workings of the class on to SR metals, passing west of Wimbledon with the 1020 Didcot-Chessington inter-regional service. On this dull autumn morning, the slight foreshortening with a telephoto lens has helped to lift the picture from the ordinary, helped by the snaking of the coal wagons, the EMU and, on the right, engineer's wagons. *Colin Marsden*

1988

12 February

We looked earlier at the decline and demise of British Rail workshops and the fate of Swindon in particular. One of the legacies of Brunel's vision and drive was the famed 'A' Shop, and for many the abandonment and subsequent demolition of this was criminal. As can be seen from this view taken from a passing train, it is fast becoming a shell, and literally a case of 'how are the mighty fallen'! A comparative view in 2005 would show not the previous wide expanse of railway land, but car parks and new housing. *Ray Ruffell*

4 March

Yet another example of turning limited pictorial components into a much more memorable shot, by choice of vantage point and inclusion of available structures: the buffer stop, being placed in the dominant bottom right 'third', creates a dramatic image that encourages the eye to dwell on the overall picture and then to study its component parts. Captured on this photographer's Nikon FM camera, on Ilford FP4 film set to 1/30th second at f16. No 142062 stands in Colne station, waiting to form the 1614 stopping service to Preston. Once the meeting point for L&YR (from Accrington) and MR (from Skipton) metals, the latter route closed on 2 February 1970, truncating what had previously provided a through route and heralding the arrival of the buffer stop seen here. *Tom Heavyside*

1988

In the very latter days of the 1980s, the service between Waterloo and Bournemouth, electrified some 20 years earlier, was converted from loco-hauled to EMU operation. Not many months before this transformation and the arrival of swish new Class 442 units, BR(SR) electro-diesel No 73105 fights a rearguard action with the 1000 Bournemouth-Waterloo service, providing the on-board travellers with the luxury of eight coaches. Resplendent with its *Quadrant* nameplates high on the bodyside, affixed the previous November at Waterloo station, the train is passing Lyndhurst Road. Note the course of an old road on either side of the tracks and the obvious abandonment of the resultant level crossing – and that what could have been the old station master's house has its nearside windows boarded up.

Later in the day, the photographer has moved south, to capture No 73129 *City of Winchester* speeding through New Milton station with another up train, this time the 1339 Bournemouth-Waterloo 'fast'. Note the happy retention of some station furniture at this location, especially the attractive footbridge, original station buildings and the provision of a sensible bike-shed! A lady scoots her way towards this facility, presumably about to take a shopping trip to Bournemouth. *Both Tom Heavyside*

1988

▲ 18 April

Not only has Brian Morrison captured some of the variety of environment surrounding London's railways – and he has used them well – but he has also captured here, near Dartford, three distinct styles of SR EMU numbering and livery. Left to right, they are: Class 415/1 4EPB No 5045 in blue/grey at the rear of the 1637 Holborn Viaduct-Dartford via Bexleyheath service, with the number centrally above the route indicator; Class 411/5 4CEP No 1566 forming a Victoria-Sidcup-Dover Priory service, which has the number above each cab window and is in beige/brown 'Jaffa cake' livery; and newly refurbished Class 423 4CEP No 3194 in NSE livery, leading the 1700 Gillingham-Cannon Street via Woolwich Arsenal service, looking rather bare with the single number just visible below the grab rail beneath the driver's cab window. *Brian Morrison*

▲ 25 April

An oft-recorded location and equally photographed motive power, but a far from ordinary train: skirting Horse Cove, Dawlish, No 50045 *Achilles* heads westward with an Exeter-Plymouth Breakdown Train Unit, complete with long-serving crane next to the engine. Note the 207 milepost on the left, showing the distance from London, the substantial tunnel mouth protecting the track from the sandstone cliff, the empty beach and the reasonably high tide. *Colin Marsden*

▼ 6 May

In a totally different scene, but no less interesting or pleasing, Blackburn station's trainshed and the play of light and shadow that this creates in the early summer sunshine, together with the tight knot of intending travellers and the approaching Class 150/2 'Sprinter' DMU No 150241, all combine to make the picture. The ancient wall-suspended clock displays the time of arrival of the 1152 service from Leeds to Blackpool North. The handling of exposure and the clarity of image make this a highly attractive scene. *Tom Heavyside*

▲ 13 May

Another Class 142 and another signal gantry produce another cleverly posed photograph. Entering Llandudno station, past the time-honoured and impressive signal box, No 142056 reaches its destination as the 1356 service from Llandudno Junction. As seen in other parts of the UK, the '142s' attempted to usurp the reign of 'heritage' DMUs, but ended up unsuccessful. *Tom Heavyside*

▼ 21 May

Despite there being nominally standard designs adopted by many of the former railway companies, virtually every signal box was unique in some feature. Whether it was the geographical location, the tight or restricted site access, or other constructional considerations, the sheer variety went a long way to enhance past railway photographs. Snodland, on the former SE&CR Maidstone-Rochester branch, was no exception. Dating back to the 1870s, it possessed 26 levers with an S. E. Brady 5-inch frame and also boasted the slim extension, originally a corridor to give some protection to the incumbent on his travels to operate the level crossing gates, but by 1988 in use as a greenhouse! Approaching it – and the station – is Class 416/4 2EPB No 6404, forming the 1444 Maidstone West-Strood service. *Brian Morrison*

▲ 28 May

From their introduction in the 1960s, for WCML express passenger duties, the Class 50s progressively garnered affection among enthusiasts and, towards the end of their lives, attracted much devotion in the 'gricer' fraternity, intent on travelling as many miles as possible behind their beloved locos. All 50 members of the class had this devotion lavished on them, but one more than any other had, for a short time, the lion's share of attention. Originally D449 and fresh from Vulcan Foundry on 11 December 1968 – three months after the end of steam on BR – No 50049 received its *Defiance* name at Laira depot on 2 May 1978, and thereafter ran as just one more of the class until celebrity status was thrust upon it. On 9 August 1987 it received special trial attention to convert it for use as a freight loco. Becoming No 50149 and

the first to wear Railfreight General livery decals, it retained its name but was transferred to less glamorous duties. The experiment was not a huge success, however, and it was renumbered to 50049 on 22 February 1989. Thereafter it continued to pick up what work it could and finally bowed out on 16 August 1991, from Laira. Here, at Dawlish, it pilots fellow '50' No 50042 *Triumph*, which certainly was not living up to its name this day, having developed a fault at Exeter. The train is the 1305 Paddington-Paignton, which No 50149 had joined at Exeter. *Colin Marsden*

▼ 31 May

When the Glanrhyd bridge on the Heart of Wales Line was swept away in the autumn floods of 19 October 1987, Llandovery became the temporary southern rail terminus for the line from the north, the onward connection to Llandeilo being made by bus. Here, Cardiff DMU set No C853 (with Driving Motor Composite W51808 leading and an unmatched centre trailer car) waits at Llandovery for the bus to arrive from Swansea, after which it will serve as the 1921 service to Crewe. This tragedy could have spelled the end of the route in other times, but in the early weeks after the accident the line's support body – the Heart of Wales Line Travellers Association (HOWLTA) – fearful of the possible death knell, pulled out all the stops to support traffic and travellers and held BR to its promise that 'the line will not be closed. The bridge will be repaired.' *MJS*

▲ 4 June

More semaphores and their controlling signal box, and what a difference they make to the picture: without them, the image would have so much less impact. With the extensive spread of rails into sidings and platform lines, it is easy to see the importance that Morecambe once enjoyed. Now, although sadly not the grandiose place it once was, it still has charisma in this shot, with the elderly DMU set strategically placed to complete the scene. Class 104 units Nos 53468 and 53494 arrive at their destination forming the 1743 local service from Lancaster. Originally numbered 50468 in January 1958 and 50494 in August 1957, the latter, the elder of the two, lasted slightly longer than its sibling, being withdrawn in June 1990 and, happily, preserved. By comparison, No 53468 was dispensed with in September 1989 and soon went to Vic Berry's yard, where it was cut up in the December. *Tom Heavyside*

▼ 15 June

Here is another picture full of interest: 'large logo' No 37427 – named *Bont y Bermo* at Barmouth on 13 April 1986 – negotiates Sandbach Junction with the 1400 Cardiff-Manchester Piccadilly 'inter-regional' service. It boasts only four carriages, but still twice the length that would later be enjoyed by these services following 'Sprinterisation'! Originally D6988, from Vulcan Foundry on 14 June 1965, it became No 37288 under TOPS in March 1974, before being fitted with ETH and converted to 37427 on 6 February 1986. A change of name – to *Highland Enterprise* – came at Inverness on 17 May 1993, but even that did not last long, being stripped some three years later. In 2005 it was allocated to Toton depot. Note the lines on the right, heading towards Middlewich and an alternative route to Manchester, and the presence of on-track plant machines in the background. *Tom Heavyside*

▲ 18 June

Apart from the livery, this view could almost have been taken at any time in the previous three decades, following the introduction of the Class 31s from Brush in the late 1950s. However, the photographer was indeed fortunate on this day, as the presence of the loco-hauled train was in place of a failed 'Sprinter' DMU! Framed by 'period piece' semaphore signals, No 31448 arrives at Blackpool North with the 1720 train from Manchester Victoria. Introduced on 19 November 1959 as D5566 and allocated to Stratford, this '31' was initially No 31148 under TOPS, but that changed on 22 August 1984, with conversion to 31448, and again, on 21 May 1990, to 31548. In this guise, with its freight turns having largely dried up or been given to competing loco types, it was in store at the end of the 20th century. *Tom Heavyside*

▼ 21 June

BR's Class 03 shunters never gained much of the limelight and often 'slid between the cracks' as far as photographers were concerned, with the slight exception of the handful in South Wales towards the end of their existence. Part of the reason may have been that they so often operated away from the normal public gaze and, not infrequently, in industrial sites where larger locos were not suited. D2162 was new from BR Swindon on 21 September 1960, to York shed, and for the ensuing decade it stayed in the NER. Eventually it saw transfer to Birkenhead, from where it was withdrawn, as No 03162, on 23 May 1989. Here it is in gainful employment, crossing Duke Street, Birkenhead, with Whitbread's 'Royal Duke Hotel' behind. The shunter rides the steps, while a guard protects the road and the driver watches his progress backwards. The loco has obviously become some sort of celebrity, being painted with its original number and graced with the legend 'Birkenhead South 1879-1985', the date most certainly not referring to the locomotive! *Tom Heavyside*

▲ 24 June
Another '31' working passenger diagrams in the North West: leaning into the very slight curve at Bromley Cross station, No 31453 is yet another DMU substitute, here forming the 1805 Blackburn-Manchester stopper. Note, on the left-hand platform, the twin signs for competing services – BR and the local Metro – plus, on the other platform, the smartened-up original station buildings, making for a pleasant juxtaposition to the train. *Tom Heavyside*

▼ 24 June
While Tom Heavyside was out and about in the North West, this photographer was much further south and closer to home as, on the same day, he captured No 50149 at Cockwood Harbour on the 1535 St Blazey-Exeter 'Speedlink' service, undertaking some of the sort of work for which it was converted. This view across the harbour is popular with photographers and, even with the tide out, the beached boats add to the charm of the picture. *Colin Marsden*

1988

▲ 13 June

By the end of the decade Class 33s were increasingly being displaced from their normal routine duties and sights such as this became much less common. No 33115 stands in Platform 3 at Salisbury, coupled to Class 438 4TC No 8017, waiting to form the 1729 service to Waterloo. At this time No 33115 was just another humdrum member of the class, but by the beginning of 1990 – having been withdrawn from capital stock in May 1989 – it achieved some notoriety by being converted at RFS Engineering in Doncaster for speed collection trials in connection with proposed Channel Tunnel locomotives. Based at Stewarts Lane and unpowered, it did, nevertheless, retain its engine as ballast weight. It was fitted with 750-volt DC shoe gear for power transfer to specially converted 'ED' No 73205 and was renumbered 83301. *MJS*

▼ 30 June

Although the engine shed was a source of delight in steam days, with myriads of photographs to prove it, the facilities for diesel and/or electrics became progressively less fascinating after 1968. Apart from the absence of the steam locomotive, which had inherent aesthetic qualities lacking in modern traction, the systematic abandonment of much of the old architecture – often not suited to more modern operations – led to vistas much depleted of interest. This photographer has not forgotten his roots, however, and here presents a view of the old steam shed at Chester, still in use at this time for DMUs. Peering over the proliferation of Royal Mail vans, we are presented with at least three different classes of DMU, a Derby Lightweight inside the building and Class 108 and 101 twins outside. Sadly, even this facility has since been dispensed with. *Tom Heavyside*

▲ 30 June

Bridges can often be a source of splendour in a photograph, especially if they have inherent design merit. While perhaps not having the same aesthetic quality as Brunel's magnificent Royal Albert Bridge across the Tamar, connecting Plymouth with Cornwall, the neighbouring road bridge, with its name and building date boldly stated on the supporting pillar, provides a fine backdrop to No 50149, again captured in its early days on freight. With the front end of the train just within Devon, the locomotive passes the 1908 Royal Albert Bridge signal box, which, although no longer used as such, was still occasionally occupied by Permanent Way gangs. *Colin Marsden*

▼ 2 July

As the end of the decade approached, the spreading tentacles of Network SouthEast reached ever outwards, stretching far outside the normal accepted parameters of that name. The NSE livery was also revised and extended to classes of motive power not originally chosen or expected to be included. One such was WCML electric No 86401, seen here passing Preston – way beyond any perceived NSE boundaries! – with a northbound train of empty steel coil flats. A little short of a year after this shot, the loco was named *Northampton Town* at Northampton on 13 May 1989, in connection with enhanced direct services from Euston. Later it received *Hertfordshire Rail Tours* nameplates, at Crewe IEMD on 14 October 1998, and was withdrawn from service in the last weeks of 2004. Note the rather disinterested spotters on the left! *Tom Heavyside*

1988

20 July

Here is Cockwood Harbour again, but this time seen from the south of the bay, to witness unbranded InterCity-liveried No 47620 *Windsor Castle* appropriately hauling the Royal Train on its way to Paignton as the 1300 departure from Paddington. Some 15 years later there was much talk in political circles as to the cost/benefit analysis of having such a train with, supposedly, a low level of use against its cost. Happily, sense prevailed and, at the time of writing, it has been reprieved, although with its exclusivity possibly diluted somewhat. Converted to this state from No 47070 on 20 September 1984 – and receiving its prestigious name ten months later at Paddington – the loco was renumbered 47835 on 8 August 1989. Another change came on 11 May 1995, with renumbering to 47799. Still designated for Royal duties, it was painted in a livery to match the claret-coloured coaches and graced with *Prince Henry* nameplates, at Wolverton. The 21st century, however, saw it in store. *Colin Marsden*

▲ 24 July

The temptation here might have been to stand either on the sloping end of the platform or on the low railings in the foreground, but that would have both restricted the angle of view and possible depth of field, and created a very ordinary record shot. However, the photographer has lifted the image by stepping back to include railings, platform end and the delightful architectural detail of the station building. No 50022 *Anson* stands in Platform 3 at Hereford at precisely 1611, waiting to set off with the 1615 Sunday service to Paddington. With the traveller chatting to a friend at the window of the leading coach and others casually standing on both platforms, there is a relaxed air about the scene that complements the image. *David Holmes*

▼ 30 July

Once more the assiduous use of station furniture, especially the split canopies at Matlock station, together with the inherent interest of the various people on the platform – some seemingly interested in the train and others not – and inclusion of 'The Paxton Buffet' notice, creates a picture rather than a mere snapshot. The DMU is also of interest. Another of the 'experimental' types which hopefully would replace the ageing 'heritage' units, the two Class 151s emerged from Metro-Cammell's works in February 1985 ('001') and January 1986 ('002'). Often employed on the Matlock branch from Derby, they were not wholly successful – although with distinct aesthetic qualities absent from other new types. Three-car units, they were renumbered '003' and '004' respectively in February 1988 so as not to clash with the Class 150/0 units, also Derby-based, that carried numbers 150001 and 150002. They were sold on to Endeavour Rail in October 1990. *Ray Ruffell*

▲ 4 August

Capturing an image from a mirror is, of course, nothing new, but the results are more often than not interesting and successful. In this view at Kilwinning station, the reversal of image is just apparent in the back-to-front '1' on the platform sign, but EMU No 318362 is far enough away for its number to be so insignificant as not to disturb the visual effect. The 1152 Largs-Glasgow service slows for this station stop, nicely framed by the substantial footbridge. *Tom Heavyside*

▼ 5 August

The following day the photographer is obviously still enjoying his stay in Scotland as he captures Nos 37055 and 37107 heading north through West Kilbride with a Ravenscraig-Hunterston train of iron ore empties. New as D6755 on 21 September 1962 and allocated to the purpose-built diesel depot at Thornaby (51L), the leading '37' spent much of its life in the North East, eventually gaining some recognition by being name *Rail Celebrity* at Toton on 15 November 1995. Sadly, it was in store by the early 21st century. By comparison, No 37107 – new as D6807 to Sheffield Darnall (41A) on 23 January 1963 – spent a large chunk of its existence in the Sheffield/South Yorkshire area, being unofficially named *Fury* at Tinsley on 17 November 1989, before being withdrawn, stored as unserviceable, in October 1999. *Tom Heavyside*

▲ 9 August

We have already seen the influx of the NSE livery, the result of former ScotRail boss Chris Green's moves to create a corporate identity for, predominantly, the lines in the south-east of the UK. This 'brave new livery' literally burst on to the scene, almost without warning, as a colourful transformation of both rolling-stock and stations, to much comment – mostly complimentary – from enthusiast and traveller alike. The initial design went through a couple of minor adjustments, but despite Privatisation in 1995 and the resultant 'coats of many colours' among the new TOCs, there were still signs of the NSE around in 2005! Even in black and white, DMU set No L409 (with Pressed Steel Class 117 DMBS No 51344 nearest the camera) looks far more presentable and attractive than the previous blue and grey. The unit is standing at Pangbourne while working the 1741 Oxford-Paddington local. *MJS*

▼ 10 August

Again using attractive elements of station architecture, Ray Ruffell has created a pleasing image of 4VEP EMU No 3103 standing in Platform 1 at Bognor Regis, awaiting departure for London Victoria. Initially No 7803 when new in December 1969, the 3103 identity was received in July 1987, but this was very short-lived, as three of the cars were reformed into set 3462 in February 1989, with DMBS No 62264 going to set 3465 one month later. Note the ample provision of waiting cover and seats, and the regularly spaced pipes for replenishing drinking water on the trains. *Ray Ruffell*

1988

▲ 16 August

Such has been the success in increasing demand on many lines throughout the country, despite Mrs Thatcher's attempt to stifle rail travel and the lack of adequate investment through successive Governments, that extra trains constantly have to be introduced, totally confounding the doom-mongers of the early 1980s. Part of this, of course, has been due to the rapid growth in road traffic and the resultant gridlock and congestion chaos, but is also against a background of constantly increasing rail fares. One such extra train on the former GWR main line was the 1807 Paddington-Swindon, introduced in May 1988. Virtually the only scheduled loco-hauled train on the route at the time, demand continued to grow, causing the service to be extended to Bristol. When still only travelling to Swindon, No 47551 heads into the lengthening sun as it passes the site of Uffington station. Note the attractive lattice road bridge in the background. Built in 1897, it was replaced exactly 100 years later – with an ugly, slab-sided version having no redeeming aesthetic features whatsoever! *MJS*

▼ 10 September

There have been many anomalies on Britain's railways, not least the running of NSE services to Exeter and Great Malvern – not exactly the south-east in either case! One of the former route's trains is here seen through a large 300mm telephoto lens departing from Waterloo, with a Class 50 still clinging to the run along the former LSWR route via Salisbury. Threatened by Class 47s at this time, No 50048 *Dauntless* winds out of the London terminus with the 1100 Exeter St David's service, with one blue and grey coach somewhat spoiling the otherwise complete set of NSE-liveried carriages and loco. Named at Reading on 16 March 1978, *Dauntless* ended stored and unserviceable at Laira on 15 July 1991. *Brian Morrison*

▲ 14 September

Many of the first generation of WCML electrics did not survive the closing years of the decade, but a handful were retained for carriage shunting duties at Euston. Having been through the carriage washing plant regularly each day, No 83009 is now almost white and looking a very sorry sight at the terminus buffer stop. Built as E3032 and released from Vulcan Foundry in November 1960, it suffered – together with others of the class – from problems with the mercury arc rectifier and was placed in store as early as 1968-71, pending refurbishment at Doncaster Works. Prior to transfer to Euston, No 83009 spent two years as a mobile transformer at Longsight depot. It lasted just six months beyond this view, being withdrawn on 19 March 1989. *MJS*

▼ 1 October

The mid-Wales route to Aberystwyth experienced see-sawing fortunes for many years, with a constant threat of closure hanging over it, but ended the decade with a commitment to retention of services and hope for the re-introduction of through trains to London. One such – and still loco-hauled at this time by engines not often seen on London-bound passenger turns elsewhere in the country – was the 1010 Aberystwyth-Euston, seen approaching Sutton Bridge Junction, Shrewsbury. No 37680 (refurbished from No 37224 in April 1987) leads No 37684 (similarly converted from No 37134 in March 1987). *Tom Heavyside*

▲ 9 October

One of the undoubted highlights of 1988, certainly from the enthusiasts' point of view, was the occasion of the very first Bescot Depot Open Day. Despite dismal or even very wet weather, depending on the time of day, visiting crowds were both numerous and enthusiastic. As well as in and around the depot buildings themselves, locos and units were lined up in the adjacent sidings. A juxtaposition of these two traction types can be seen here, with a new Class 90 on the extreme right, next to a Class 310 unit of longer standing but with new credentials. No 310101, built as 310073 in February 1966 at Derby Works, has just undergone refurbishment and re-classification to Standard Class-only at Wolverton the previous month. Initially serving the West Midlands area in this new state, the Class 310/1s were displaced in the early 1990s by Class 323s and they moved south to East Ham, following the migration to the LTS by unrefurbished class members in 1988. *MJS*

◄ 30 October

As well as cutting locos and units and stripping asbestos, Vic Berry also undertook repainting for both BR and LUT, winning, in the process, an enviable reputation for the quality of the finished product. Obviously needing clean conditions for this, the purpose-built paint sheds were not the most comfortable of places to work, with tight, cramped conditions. No 31130 is here masked around the windows and below the bodyside and in yellow undercoat, ready for its shiny new coat to be applied. One of the Crewe nuclear flask pool, this was the second of this sub-Sector to be dealt with by Vic, following No 31275, which had been completed in appropriate Railfreight livery earlier in the month. *MJS*

▲ 6 November

One of the instructions to its photographers by *National Geographic* magazine was to include people in the shots. 'If there is not one handy, use your family' seems to be the message here, as the photographer poses his daughter Margaret at Dartford to add glamour and counterbalance to the two units monopolising the left-hand side of the picture. The actual train workings are unrecorded, but No 5231 is bound for Charing Cross, Cannon Street or Holborn Viaduct, while No 5493 is heading for Gravesend or even Gillingham. Class 415/1 4EPB No 5231, a four-car set new in August 1956, was withdrawn in May 1991 and immediately cut up at Booth Roe Metals, Rotherham. Class 415/4 4EPB No 5493, by comparison, initially a three-car set in August 1952 as No 5014 and augmented to four cars by 1948-vintage TS No 15014, was renumbered in October 1986, following which it was withdrawn in February 1993 and cut seven months later by Gwent Demolition Co alongside the yard of Margam depot. *Ray Ruffell*

▼ 23 November

The introduction of 'Sprinters' was supposed to be the answer to many prayers, but they were not to be without their problems! Class 155s, especially, caused serious headaches by having door malfunctions shortly after entering service, and the whole class was temporarily withdrawn from service on Friday 16 December 1988. Only three weeks earlier, No 155308, just one year old, is seen in the bay Platform 3 at Oxford station, still looking very clean and smart, shortly before leaving as the 2018 service to Worcester. In common with all but seven of the Leyland '155s' retained by West Yorkshire PTE, the two-car sets were split into single units and reclassified as Class 153; No 155308 became 153358 in October 1991 and 153308 one month later. *MJS*

▲ 23 November

The development of Sectorisation on BR dictated that all manner of operating areas were 'owned' by various Sectors of the organisation. This even extended to particular services, with the North East-South West sub-Sector of InterCity supervising this 1528 Poole-Liverpool train. No 47663, pausing in Platform 2 at Oxford with its ten-coach train, was previously No 47240, being renumbered in January 1987 under BR's ETH conversion programme. Just three months after this view, on 21 February 1989, it changed yet again, this time to 47818, complete with long-distance fuel tanks; in that guise it was named *Strathclyde* at Polmadie depot on 16 September 2000. Sadly, the honour was reversed on 31 March 2003! *MJS*

▼ 28 November

The 'East Coast Revival' – the £517million electrification of the ECML – was the largest single investment on BR for some considerable time and was completed between London and Edinburgh in the summer of 1991. The route to Leeds, however, was energised from October 1988, and much play was made of the corresponding launch of the InterCity 225 'Electras' from GEC. They were to be the flagship of the line, bringing main-line push-pull operations to the capital, with Class 82 Mk 4 DVTs at the opposite end of the train from the '91'. They were all considered to be the way for the future! On a driver training special, No 91008, just four months old, looks the part and solicits interested glances from members of the public as it waits to take the road to Peterborough. Shame about the old-liveried Mk 3 stock behind it, however! *Colin Marsden*

Despite much electrification and re-signalling throughout the country, there were pockets where old practices survived. Apart from the locomotive – although even this is in mock GWR green – this view is timeless, with a ballast train, semaphore signals and a railman attending to the signal lamps, oil can in hand. Complete with brass cabside numbers and BR 'double-arrow' logo, as well as the green coat, applied for the GW150 celebrations, No 47628 *Sir Daniel Gooch* approaches High Wycombe with an up works ballast train. *MJS*

▼ 11 December

With the re-routing of various InterCity services between London and Birmingham, Coventry gained an increased importance and a thorough mix of motive power. On the left, NSE-liveried No 47582 *County of Norfolk* pauses with the 0840 Paddington-Wolverhampton service, while on the right No 86103 *André Chapelon* passes with a Euston-Preston train. Following Privatisation and the onset of Richard Branson's 'Red Revolution', both types of motive power were eliminated from these services. Having become No 47733 on 18 August 1995, and having a name change one month later, to *Eastern Star* at York, in 2005 it was out of work. No 86103 was also in store into the 21st century, having been ousted from front-line work. *MJS*

1988

15 December

Appropriately, here is a night-time shot to close the year! The clock shows 5 o'clock, but whether that is morning or afternoon or whether it has stopped is uncertain! If the former, most of Plymouth will still be asleep as the photographer captures the quiet tranquillity of Laira depot, focusing on (left to right) No 50029 *Renown*, No 47508 *SS Great Britain* and No 50041 *Bulwark*. The two '50s' are close to the end of their active lives, being withdrawn from this depot on 25 March 1992 and 17 April 1990 respectively; whereas the '47', devoid of nameplates from October 1992, remained until 14 May 1993, withdrawn then as unserviceable from Bristol Bath Road depot. *Colin Marsden*

1989

29 January

An unexceptional picture you may think: three locomotives stand in a shed yard, not usual bedfellows possibly, but all is not what it seems. The location is Leicester depot (the former 15C steam shed) and Class 40s were most certainly not a common sight, even during WCML electrification when members of the class did make the occasional foray on to the Midland main line, but in 1989…? Here, bearing all the three numbers and name that it carried during its operational life –

212 (ex-D212), 40012, 97407 and *Aureol* – this '40', together with companion No 25173 behind, have been stripped of asbestos at nearby Vic Berry's yard and have recently arrived on shed prior to moving into preservation. No 212 was bound for the Midland Railway Centre at Butterley, while the 'Rat', once named *John F. Kennedy*, was destined for the 'The Railway Age' centre in Crewe. Beyond both, local loco No 56063 *Bardon Hill* completes the trio; built in September 1979, the '56' was stored as serviceable by 2005. *MJS*

▲ 9 February

To partly replace D200 as a 'celebrity' locomotive, when it was withdrawn in April 1988, the original Class 37, D6700, was repainted into near-original green livery at Crewe in the early months of that year. It then gained the distinction of being the last of the class to receive an intermediate overhaul at the Works. Initially carrying both D6700 and 37119 (its TOPS number), it was renumbered by the end of March 1988 to 37350, with the fitting of re-geared CP7 bogies. Working out of Cardiff Canton depot, it was normally allocated to Ripple Lane diagrams, but an alternative working was the 1120 Theale-Robeston oil train turn. One of those is seen here, double-headed as usual, with the aged machine as train engine and five-years-younger sibling No 37371 – D6847/37147 of June 1963 vintage – taking the lead. They are passing the remains of Challow station on the GWR main line on their way to Wales. *MJS*

▼ 17 February

As if to prove that attractive photographs are possible in less than ideal conditions – and that you should never put your camera away! – this photographer has made excellent use of rain, lights, reflections and a slow shutter speed to capture No 43074 dramatically powering up at King's Cross as it prepares to leave the station on a down express. Surrounding it and awaiting their departures for the north are, left to right, unique Brush-designed No 89001 *Avocet*, No 43197 – later to achieve special status by being named *Railway Magazine Centenary 1897-1997* at Plymouth station on 22 November 1996 – and No 43121 (the former *West Yorkshire Metropolitan County*). *Brian Morrison*

▲ 4 March

This delightful portrait shows something that was once so common but which seemed to vanish so rapidly – and is now gone without trace. By their very design, it is clear that the Class 20s were a product of the 1955 Modernisation scheme, inheriting the basic steam engine shape of cab at one end and longish 'boiler' in front. This design militated against some of their operations, leading to the frequent use of a pair 'nose to nose', as here, so that there was effectively a cab at each end for travel is either direction. Diverted from the WCML to run a circuitous route from Carnforth to Preston via Hellifield, Nos 20058 and 20087 haul a Ravenscraig-Shotton steel coil train through Clitheroe, bounded on either side by rows of terrace housing. *Tom Heavyside*

▼ 11 March

During more recent years there has been much comment and railway press coverage of the desecration wrought on Blackburn's station. Together with changing traffic patterns, there was also consideration of maintenance costs, etc, but the decision to strip away the long-standing trainshed was met with almost universal opposition locally. While it was not a thing of overwhelming beauty, it did nevertheless provide considerable protection for waiting passengers and the subsequent provision has been far less satisfactory. No 142012 is seen working the 0920 Colne-Blackpool service, though judging by the number of photographers at this end of the platforms, this is probably not to be the main focus of attention this morning! *Tom Heavyside*

14 March

As in the King's Cross photograph on page 102, rain has here been used to enhance the view, utilising the reflections to add depth, dimension and drama to this otherwise standard portrait of EMU set No 304005 entering Platform 13 of Manchester Piccadilly with the 1230 service to Crewe. A common sight and an ordinary photograph at the time, the remaining examples of these ageing EMUs were progressively withdrawn from the early 1990s. No 304005, once a four-car set but here reduced to three after the scrapping of TS No 70049 in 1986, was one of the later ones to survive, finally succumbing to the inevitable in December 1994. Cutting was undertaken at MC Metal Processing's yard in Glasgow in May 1996.

By the end of our decade plans were well advanced for a series of 'light' railways in and around Manchester, part of which would affect the terminal platforms at Manchester Victoria. Unaware of the fate awaiting it, this area of the station gives temporary refuge to 'Pacer' unit No 142051 (No 55701 leading), waiting to form the 1110 service to Rochdale via Oldham. By the expression on the ganger's face, it may be that he is aware of the plans and is fearful for his job! Subsequently, not only were these platforms to be affected, but the entire service that this train is about to handle was axed late in 2004, in readiness for replacement by an expanding Metro system. However, the Strategic Rail Authority then pulled the plug on funding, leaving the route in uncertainty. *Both MJS*

14 March

In those same suburban platforms at Manchester Victoria, a prospective passenger prepares to stow his bicycle aboard Class 504 Manchester-Bury DC EMU No M65457. In Metro orange livery, it will leave as the 1144 stopping service to Bury. When the LRT system was developed in 1991/2, these platforms were swept away and most of the units assigned to the scrap heap.

Of all the many and varied liveries that BR adopted during the 1980s, none was more irritating to both enthusiasts and railmen alike than the InterCity version with microscopic loco numbers. Causing concern and complaints from both factions, these numbers were not easy to read even at close range, when the engine was stationary, as amply demonstrated by No 87005 *City of London* as it rests at the buffer stop in Manchester Piccadilly station. Thankfully – and happily for the sanity of all concerned! – common sense prevailed and larger numbers reappeared, bringing yet more livery variety! *Both MJS*

23 March

This is another image that is not all it appears to be. In a period when DMUs were being replaced by new-generation 'Sprinter' stock – which was late in delivery! – and the former WR had to make do with whatever was available, the 1050 Paignton-Cardiff service is here formed of two half-brake vehicles, providing just one carriage's capacity of compartment stock for this not insignificant journey! No 50005 *Collingwood* is decidedly overpowered and underworked and attracts little more than the photographer's sole attention as it heads away from Dawlish station and passes the 206 milepost. The loco's withdrawal, from Laira depot, came on 11 December 1990. *Colin Marsden*

26 March

As has been already recorded, the sight of Class 20s on rostered freight trains was becoming a thing of the past as the decade drew to a close. On this date, despite the time of year, the sun was hot and high, creating a feeling of lethargy, a condition echoed in the easy pace of Nos 20157 and 20007, seen from the old steam shed yard, as they leave the confines of Leicester's London Road station and head north on the Midland main line. Somewhat incredibly, No 20007, one of the very early examples of the class – new on 19 September 1957 – was still on the official books, although stored unserviceable at Bescot, at the close of the 20th century, whereas its classmate seen here was withdrawn, from Toton, on 10 October 1990!

Ah, happy days! On the same day, in another part of the old steam shed yard at Leicester, the depot was home to a surprisingly varied line-up. Left to right are Nos 31185, 47320, 56061, 46023 (alias Departmental 97402) and DMU set L101 (the Old Oak-allocated route-learning car Departmental No TDB975023, the former W55001). With the latter, of Class 122, already withdrawn (and since preserved) and a never-ending push towards greater standardisation, views such as this became ever rarer in these late years of the decade and beyond. *Both MJS*

▲ 30 March

As time ticked by, first-generation DMUs became more popular and acquired a genuine following, not least among photographers. With withdrawals and accident damage, there were many reformations of sets and it was often difficult to keep pace with developments. Remarkably stable at this time, however, was Reading set L842, and it achieved some notoriety on 19 November 1988 when it was despatched to work the Ashford-Hastings service in place of DEMU No 205018, which had suffered a traction motor failure. Sadly, the DMU itself failed at Staplehurst! At Pangbourne, working the 1741 Oxford-Paddington service, it is carrying a misleading destination blind! The front and rear cars of this Class 101 set – Nos 53314 and 53327 respectively – were both new in March

1958, whereas the centre car, No 59101, was slightly older, dating from November 1957, and was renumbered 59110 13 months after this view. Withdrawn in December 1995, it was cut at MC Metals' Glasgow yard the same month. *MJS*

▼ 8 April

Another location that has seen much change and rationalisation over the years is Buxton. This view has been totally transformed in that locos are no longer berthed here, but out in the country at Peak Forest. On this day, however, there is a healthy contingent present, as No 150225 leaves the former LNWR station with the 1307 stopper to Manchester Piccadilly. Standing on shed are, left to right, Nos 47186, 37687 and 37676. *Tom Heavyside*

▲ 13 April

One of the most successful innovations in our period was the 'Thameslink' service, running through trains from Brighton to Bedford across the River Thames. Class 319 EMUs handled the services great success and in the NSE livery were very attractive. Here No 319056 departs from Clapham Junction with the 1640 Victoria-Brighton train, one of the handful of services that stayed south of the river. Design ideas changed during our decade with, thankfully, aesthetics playing a much greater part in the final designs, and hideous corridor ends being abandoned. New in July 1988, '056 underwent refurbishment ten years later and emerged as No 319456, for use on the newly classified 'City Flyer' Bedford-Gatwick-Brighton services. *Colin Marsden*

▼ 15 April

The use of a slightly wider-angle lens here accentuates the length of the ECML '91/DVT' sets that operated the main routes out of King's Cross, but in truth the trains were quality products, providing passengers with space and luxury. This attention to customer needs has made GNER, which inherited the route at Privatisation in 1995, one of the most successful of the TOCs, far outshining many of its often higher-profile contemporaries. No 91007, named in honour of *Ian Allan* on 21 October 1992 at Leeds, brings up the rear of the 1700 Leeds-King's Cross express, as it pauses for custom at Wakefield (Westgate) station. *Tom Heavyside*

▲ 6 May

Another 'trademark' image from this photographer once again makes great use of the surrounding 'props', and breaks all the rules by separating us from the train by a dry-stone wall and closed gate, yet still producing a super view. Seen at Strickland, between Penrith and Shap, an unidentified Class 90 heads south with the 1744 Edinburgh-Birmingham express, made up of six Mk 3 coaches and a blue and grey Brake, threading its way through the landscape so typical of this part of the UK. *Tom Heavyside*

◄ 21 May

In the past it was just steam excursions that drew the crowds, and even since 1968 this has been largely true, but with an increasing number of people who never knew 'real' steam, modern traction has become ever more popular. A delightful innovation and highlight of 1989 was the InterCity Diesel Day, organised by Hertfordshire Railtours, where a variety of trains ran between Leicester and St Pancras, hauled by most unusual motive power. As can be imagined, this was greatly appreciated by enthusiasts, especially on the day, as the weather was near perfect! Hot and sunny, some of the resultant heat haze can be seen behind No 37058 as it heads north under the wires past Sundon, north of Luton, with the 1040 out of St Pancras. Note the heads poking from the leading carriage windows, savouring every moment of the tour! *MJS*

1 June

Another innovation, following in the tradition set by the 'GW150' celebrations, was the painting of Class 47 No 97561 in Midland Railway maroon and naming it *Midland Counties Railway 150 1839-1989* on 23 May 1989. Celebrating the 150th anniversary of the birth of the Midland Railway, the loco was used by Derby Control on a number of specials over the ensuing few weeks. A mere nine days after the event – and looking magnificent in its new coat – it stands at Hellifield station, having brought a BR special from Leicester. Sadly, it lasted in this guise only a very short while, as the BR computer could not cope with this numbering; it summarily reverted to

No 47973 on 15 July and was then repainted and de-named in March 1990! Waiting patiently on the right is preserved Stanier '8F' No 48151, which took the train on to Carlisle.

The '8F' is seen here on Carlisle (Upperby) depot, receiving attention prior to hauling the return trip, while the tour participants were free to enjoy the sights and sounds of the city. Having had its smokebox emptied of ash and with coal and water replenished, it is now ready to run back with its support coach to Citadel station, looking totally at home on this former steam shed and evoking fond memories of past times. The driver poses for his portrait, while the fireman checks the coal supply. *Both MJS*

1 June

The aforementioned problems with the 'Sprinters' – door troubles and late introduction to service – led to loco-hauled substitutions on an ever-widening scale, albeit temporarily. This gave rise to some rather unusual workings, and film manufacturers must have made a tidy profit out of the extra rolls expended! Having retraced my steps from Upperby shed to Citadel station, I was blessed with this view of the three-coach 1405 service from Newcastle arriving (8 minutes late!) behind No 47501 *Craftsman*. The name was removed in 1997 and the loco withdrawn from store on 12 July 2002, but happily it was re-instated on 6 September 2003 and at the time of writing was working from Carlisle Kingmoor depot.

To complete our trip to Carlisle on this glorious sunny summer day, we take a look at yet another livery permutation. Some of the proliferation of new liveries harked back to more leisurely times and, not least, the early days of dieselisation in the 1950s. Perhaps a little way from its original stamping ground, Chester DMU set CH274, comprising Class 108 Nos E54247 and 53964, stands in Carlisle station waiting to form the 1830 service to Barrow, complete with specially applied green coat, front end 'whiskers' atop the regulation yellow, and mid-period totem on the bodyside. The former Nos 56247 and 50964 of May 1959, both coaches were withdrawn in June 1992 and cut at Booth Roe Metals in Rotherham the same month. Note the two enthusiasts, looking wistfully south – in hopeful expectation? *Both MJS*

2 June

Compare this view with that on page 62 of Volume 1 of this series, covering 1980-84, and see how much has disappeared over the ensuing seven years. With the closure of the 'Leicester Gap', the signal box at Loughborough was removed together with semaphore signals, and much of the main-line trackwork – here to the left – was rationalised. Happily, at this time, the ARC yard adjacent to the station was still very active, as can be seen, but even here, just a few years later, all was abandoned. In appropriate Railfreight Construction livery, No 56050 has come off the down main line and is backing into the yard with a rake of empties. By the end of the century, the 1978-vintage '56' had itself ceased operations and been placed into store, with the whole class extinct on normal duties early in 2004.

Yet more rationalisation was wrought on the Leicester scene in the early 1990s, with the removal of the former MR lamps from Leicester depot yard, to be replaced with huge, ugly tower structures. As can be seen, the engineer's preparations are well under way in the yard and this crop of railway 'red-hot pokers' will soon be a thing of the past. 'Skinhead' No 31102 stands among them, with an unidentified Class 56 nearby. Built as D5520 in February 1959 and named *Cricklewood* at Tinsley in January 1990, No 31102 is a remarkable survivor and was still at work in 2005! Sadly, the former steam shed yard had largely been abandoned by EWS by this time and its future was uncertain. *Both MJS*

1989

10 June

Here is another example of the totally inappropriate size of locomotive numbering! Suitably graced with an InterCity livery, No 47568 prepares to restart from Cheltenham with the 0820 Tenby-York 'InterCity Holidaymaker' service, transporting holidaymakers home from their break in South Wales. Named *Royal Engineers Postal and Courier Services* at Long Marston on 20 March 1990, this was replaced by *Royal Logistic Corps Postal & Courier Services* at MoD Bicester on 26 May 1993. This was followed by a change of number, to 47726, on 8 September 1995, and yet another

name on 24 November 1995, *Progress*, at Manchester Airport!

Another holiday special is seen at Cheltenham on the same day. These trains often brought unusual types, and this is no exception, with double-headed Class 31s certainly not being the norm, but rostered for some trains from the North West to Devon and Cornwall. No 31421 (in all-over 'Corporate Blue') leads 31455 (in brand new Departmental grey and renumbered to 31555 one year later) as they accelerate through the station with the 0918 Manchester-Paignton train. The lone traveller shows no interest whatsoever! *Both MJS*

15 June

Another lesson in how to make a picture of SR EMUs interesting! The tell-tale chimneys of Battersea Power Station and other examples of London architecture give the game away as to the location as, on the left, Class 416/3 2EPB No 6314 slows for the prescribed stop at Wandsworth Road station with the 1821 London Bridge-Victoria service. In the centre, Class 415/4 4EPB No 5459 heads towards Factory Junction, Battersea, with the 1819 Orpington-Victoria service,

while on the right Class 415/1 and 415/6 4EPBs Nos 5248 and 5601 make up the 1832 Victoria-Orpington train. In order, these units disappeared from our railway scene in July 1993 (and cut the same month at Gwent Demolition), January 1994 (cut in June 1994, again at Gwent Demolition), August 1993 (Gwent Demolition the same month) and February 1995 (as No 5602 and again at Gwent Demolition the same month). *Brian Morrison*

▲ 16 June

Here are two further lessons in how to make images more interesting. Often, what separates a quality photographer from an ordinary one is either what is put into the picture or what is left out. Here, the former applies as No 37504 *British Steel Corby* skirts Middlesbrough station in the early afternoon, with a mixed ABS freight to Thornaby. The skill here is to stand in the shadows – and not only include them, but retain detail in the darker areas, against the bright sunshine – and incorporate weeds and columns and, on the extreme right as an added bonus, a glimpse of an approaching passenger train. The attractive canopy brackets add finesse to the picture and present another feature on which the eye can rest. Its name removed a couple of years after this view, the '37' was then converted for Channel Tunnel work on 2 May 1996, becoming No 37603. *Colin Marsden*

▼ 22 June

Compared to views in the 21st century, when the powers that be were paranoid over safety and the HSE ran riot, the single 'Danger – overhead live wires' sign and rudimentary fencing seem remarkably relaxed at keeping trespassers away from the railway. The wooden structure – more stile than fence – is again used by this photographer to escape from the mundane in capturing No 86402 heading south past Coppull Moor, near Standish, between Preston and Wigan, with an up express. Converted to No 86602 for freight duties a little over four months after this shot, 2005 saw it in store at LNWR, Crewe. *Tom Heavyside*

24 June

Once again, Brian Morrison shows why he is such a successful professional transport photographer – and has been for more than half a century! Here he delightfully frames 1960-vintage Class 411/5 4CEP No 1578 and 423/0 4VEP No 3163 (much younger, from July 1973) jointly forming the 1809 Dover Priory-Victoria service at Canterbury East. The semaphore bracket helps to make the picture, but pride of place must go to the elevated former SE&CR signal box – was there perhaps special 'danger money' payment for coping with those stairs? Installed around 1911, it contained 28 levers and made a fair stab at competing aesthetically with its 1928 contemporary at Canterbury West. *Brian Morrison*

▲ 25 June

Such was the success of the four initial Class 59s that a fifth was ordered from General Motors by Foster Yeoman. Not long after its arrival, No 5 stands in the centre of the group, especially arranged for this portrait at Merehead, after being shown off during at an Open Day. Left to right, the locos are Nos 59001 *Yeoman Endeavour*, 59002 *Yeoman Enterprise*, 59005 *Kenneth J. Painter*, 59003 *Yeoman Highlander* and 59004 *Yeoman Challenger*. Perhaps surprisingly, this new fifth member of the class did not perpetuate the naming tradition of its predecessors, but was named after a member of the Foster Yeoman management team, much to Mr Painter's complete surprise when he unveiled the nameplate at the Open Day! *Colin Marsden*

▼ 8 July

This weekend saw the centenary of the coming of the railway to Chesham in Buckinghamshire. To mark the event, this Saturday and Sunday, together with the previous weekend, saw shuttles run between Chesham and Watford, with steam at one end and preserved Metropolitan electric No 12 *Sarah Siddons* at the other. This caused a great stir locally, as it had been some 25 years since steam had been seen on much of the third-rail route! Quainton Road preservation centre provided 'Metropolitan No 1' as the steam loco and the exhaust from this can be seen at the head of the 1220 returning shuttle, rounding the curve into Rickmansworth station. With the approaching steam loco being the focus of attention, the former Met battery loco No 18 in the bay platform is temporarily ignored. *MJS*

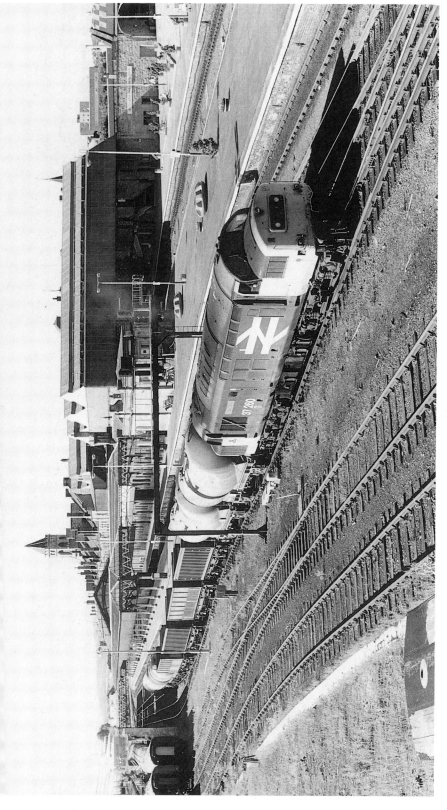

10 July

Once a great Mecca for enthusiasts, with its main-line status, a hub of branches of both Caledonian and North British origin and a sizeable engine shed to cope with all this traffic, progressive changes have drastically reduced motive power and operations at Perth, greatly diluting the appeal. Still an important station locally, despite the closure of some of the old routes, it is sadly now a shadow of its former self. Thankfully, for more general appreciation, the vast majority of the cavernous station architecture is extant and can be seen in the background as No 37260 *Radio Highland* threads its train through the avoiding lines prior to heading south with a mixed freight from Inverness. New as D6960 in January 1965 and initially allocated to Sheffield Darnall (41A), it remained an ER loco until it became an early recipient of TOPS numbering in December 1973. Thereafter, it moved north to Scotland, receiving its name at Dingwall on 6 July 1984 and finally being switched off at Inverness in August 1989, six weeks after this view. *Tom Heavyside*

11 July

One again this photographer's skill has placed the train in its context to precisely the right degree and exactly 'on spot' to create a pleasing image. With the delightful surroundings of Dalnaspidal adding to the visual feast, No 47617 *University of Stirling* heads south-east between Dalwhinnie and Blair Atholl with the 1445 Inverness-Edinburgh service. The A9 road, which follows the railway for many miles in this area, can be seen on the rising ground in the distance. Originally new in May 1964, No 47149 gained the number seen here on 24 July 1984, receiving its name just seven weeks later at Stirling station. A further transformation came on 8 July 1991, when it became No 47677, in which state it was withdrawn, stored as unserviceable, from Immingham depot on 28 January 1998. *Tom Heavyside*

▲ 31 July

The former Cambrian 'Central Wales' line from Shrewsbury to Aberystwyth and Pwllheli is one of great scenic beauty, but for railway fans over the past 20 or so years has possessed little variety of motive power. Freights are distinct highlights, but they are few and far between and, latterly, have been even scarcer than of yore, although in 2005 there were straws in the wind that may see this change. Thus this view of ageing Class 37 No 37426 *Y Lein Fach/Vale of Rheidol* arriving at Machynlleth station with an up oil train from Aberystwyth was a distinct bonus while waiting for the next DMU and brightened the dull weather conditions! The line was to receive further enhanced status into the 21st century, being chosen for trials with the new ERTMS signalling system. *MJS*

▼ 12 August

Another of this year's centenaries was that of Brush Engineering's Falcon Works in Loughborough. To celebrate the event, the company resurrected a past tradition by presenting an Open Day, graced by a visit from a descendant of the founding US family. For rail fans, however, more normally excluded from these hallowed portals, the definite centre of interest was the new build of Class 60s. Inside the finishing shop as part of the displays were (left to right) Nos 60006, 60003, 60005 and 60007, later to become *Great Gable*, *Christopher Wren*, *Skiddaw* and *Robert Adam* respectively. With the bodies built and basically painted by Procor in Rotherham, they were transhipped to Brush for fitting out and hand-over to BR. *MJS*

1989

121

◄ **12 August**

As if to prove that nothing is that permanent on our Permanent Way, or has a divine right to survive, even 'Sprinters' could be scrapped soon after introduction! Initially as part of Class 150/1 No 150112 in October 1985, coach 52212 was half of renumbered No 150212 in May 1987 before being involved in a collision. No 52209, of unit No 150209, was also involved at the contretemps at Seamer, south of Scarborough, on the former NER route to York. Both were considered beyond economic repair and condemned in April 1989, followed by a move to Vic Berry's yard and scrapping soon after. Here No 52212 is on trestles, having been robbed of its bogies and internally stripped of useful components. Having acquired unwelcome and untidy graffiti, it awaits its final fate in the Leicester scrapyard. Note the ancient steam loco behind, which was scheduled for renovation! *MJS*

◄ **6 September**

With the splitting of BR into separate financially accountable business Sectors, able to contract work wherever it was considered advantageous, all manner of strange workings could be seen around our railway system. One such, seen approaching the site of the old GWR station at Challow on the GWR main line, is Reading DMU set L409 in NSE livery, returning empty to Reading after a session of wheel turning at Cardiff Canton! With virtually all other passenger stock being HSTs on the route at this time, the sight of this 'heritage' set was a pleasant diversion. *MJS*

▲ **5 October**

A last look at Vic Berry's yard in this period – a site beloved of many enthusiasts and a source of wonder to pedestrians on the adjacent Great Central Way, but which would so dramatically disappear within just a few years (see Volumes 1 and 3 of this series for further images). Looking for all the world as if it is about to leave to handle a local train service, the former Chester DMU set CH617 is merely awaiting the cutter's torch! BRCW Class 104 No 53465, nearest the camera, emerged new as No 50465 in December 1957 and served faithfully until withdrawal in August 1989 and its final trip to Leicester. If one was to look through this bridge aperture in 2005, the view would be totally blocked by a new housing estate of dubious design value! *MJS*

▲ 23 October

It is sometimes quite amazing where former BR engines will turn up and what type they might be. Long withdrawn, May 1958-vintage Class 03 No 2022 stands in the siding serving Cooper's (Metals) Ltd in Swindon, alongside the massive Rover car plant and the former Highworth branch that brought materials into that plant. Built as No 11209, before BR decided to renumber non-steam locos with 'D' or 'E' prefixes,

it became D2022 and stayed at its original allocation of 40B (Immingham) for over a decade. It was finally withdrawn from Gateshead depot on 7 November 1982 but, thankfully, was spared destruction by being preserved at the nascent Swindon & Cricklade Railway. They in turn lent it to Cooper's, who used it to help with yet more destruction! By the end of the 20th century, it was back at Blunsdon on the S&CR and can be seen regularly by visitors. *MJS*

► 24 October

As the decade ended, the HST sets on the GWR main line had seen more than a decade of constant hard work. Logging up many hundreds of miles daily, they have proved themselves many times over and are widely recognised as being *the* best design to come out of BR since the end of steam. They were also widely appreciated by the travelling public, with passenger numbers constantly growing on their routes. Their design has aesthetic positives and this is demonstrated by power car No 43145, then bearing the latest livery, as it stands at Newport station, waiting to continue to Swansea as the 1200 out of Paddington.

They may have been approaching 'life expired' status, but due to the teething troubles with their replacements, 'heritage' DMUs were kept going at all costs in many parts of the country, often pressed into service at short notice. Having already served for 30 years, Bristol DMU set B971 is about to accumulate even more mileage, setting out as the 1247 stopping service to Abergavenny from Newport's Platform 3. The end was not far way for these sets, however, with the relentless onslaught of 'Sprinters', 'SuperSprinters' and the imminent arrival of 'Express' and 'Turbo' units. *Both MJS*

14 October

Twilight for the decade and for many more loco classes: with the sun sinking lower in the sky and the onset of night, car headlights are used to spotlight these three different classes at March depot. Left to right, they are Nos 20186 (stored unserviceable at Toton two years later and finally withdrawn on 23 July 1993), 37711 *Tremorfa Steelworks* (renovated in 1988 from No 37085, stripped of its name in 1993 and stored in the opening years of the 21st century), and 31135 (the former D5553 of 1959 and withdrawn from store on 4 February 2000). Another example of always having the camera handy and using a little imagination and ingenuity! *Brian Morrison*

▲ 1 November

Another night-time shot lit by artificial light, this time we are within the confines of a station. With exposure superbly handled, allowing detail to be captured in the shadows and clarity in the medium tones, but preventing highlights being burned out – even including the marker headlights of the loco – No 31232 stands in Platform 6 at Crewe, waiting for a driver and an addition to its train before heading south with a parcels working. New as D5659 on 20 October 1960, going first to March shed and staying on the ER for at least the next decade – apart from a four-month stay at Rugby Testing Centre in 1965 – the loco was to be in store at the age of 40. *Tom Heavyside*

▼ 6 December

The shape of (some) things to come? With plans to build 200 fully air-conditioned Class 471 'Networker Express' units as replacements for the entire Kent Coast fleet of ageing EMUs, a full-size mock-up was unveiled at Victoria station in London in the presence of Chris Green, Director of NSE, and Michael Portillo, Transport Minister. This was to gauge customer and staff reaction before the actual design was finalised. Here, the impressive front end – albeit with the retention of an ugly corridor connection – is dramatically captured during the launch. After Privatisation, the TOC that would have operated the units, Connex, was not interested in express Kent Coast stock and the Class 471s were never proceeded with, eventually being superseded by present-day Class 375 'Electrostars'. *Brian Morrison*

Index